D0404286

Arabic

English–Arabic
Arabic–English

Mahmoud Gaafar & Jane Wightwick

HIPPOCRENE BOOKS, INC.
New York

For information, address:
HIPPOCRENE BOOKS, INC.
171 Madison Avenue
New York, NY 10016
www.hippocrenebooks.com

Design and typesetting by:
g-and-w PUBLISHING, Oxfordshire, UK
www.g-and-w.co.uk

Library of Congress Cataloing-in-Publication Data

Gaafar, Mahmoud.
    Arabic : English-Arabic, Arabic-English /
Mahmoud Gaafar & Jane Wightwick.
        p. cm. -- (Hippocrene's compact series)
        ISBN-10: 0-7818-1044-2
        ISBN-13: 978-0-7818-1044-9
        1. Arabic language--Dictionaries--English.
2. English language--Dictionaries--Arabic.
I. Wightwick, Jane. II. Title. III. Series.

PJ6640.G318 2004
492.7'321--dc22

                                        2004052313

Printed in the United States of America.

CONTENTS

INTRODUCTION

Hippocrene's *Compact Arabic Dictionary* will provide you with a pocket-sized reference whether you are traveling in the Arabic-speaking world or simply want a portable dictionary for your studies.

The most common Arabic words are included in the two-way English–Arabic, Arabic–English dictionary. We have used a simplified and functional form of Modern Standard Arabic that can be understood in all Arab countries.

In addition, there is a handy introduction to pronunciation and the Arabic alphabet, together with a verb appendix showing how the different types of verbs are conjugated.

ARABIC PRONUNCIATION

The pronunciation in this dictionary is designed to be intuitive. It emphasizes simplicity at the expense of the more subtle Arabic sounds, which can only be properly mastered with time and further study. Remember that the most important thing for you is to be understood.

Many Arabic sounds are familiar and similar to their English equivalents – see Arabic Alphabet on page 9. However, there are some unfamiliar sounds that benefit from additional explanation:

Arabic letter	Pronunciation
خ *kh*	throaty **h** as in the Yiddish **ch**utzpah or the Scottish lo**ch**
ث *th*	soft **th** as in **th**in, often pronounced as **t** or **s** in colloquial dialects

Arabic letter	Pronunciation
ذ *dh*	hard **th** as in **th**at, often pronounced as **z** in colloquial dialects
غ *gh*	throaty **r** as in the French **r**ue
ح *H*	breathy **h**, as if breathing on glasses to clean them
ج *j*	soft **j** as in the French **j**e. Pronounced **g** as in **g**ate in Northern Egypt
ص *S*	emphatic **s** (pronounced with the tongue touching the roof the mouth)
ض *D*	emphatic **d**
ط *T*	emphatic **t**
ظ *DH*	emphatic **dh**, often pronounced as an emphatic **d** in colloquial dialects

Arabic letter	Pronunciation
ع '	the letter 'ain (ع) is difficult for beginners to reproduce. It is a strangulated **ah** sound. We have not rendered the 'ain directly in the pronunciation, but used an apostrophe ('). To achieve basic communication in Arabic, it is not necessary to reproduce the 'ain. The context of the sentence will help you to be understood.

THE ARABIC ALPHABET

On pages 8–9 you will find the Arabic letters in alphabetical order. The script is written from *right to left* and most Arabic letters join to the following letter in a word. This usually affects the shape of the letter. The chart shows how the letters look at the beginning, in the middle, and at the end of a word.

letter sound	beginning	middle	end
alif *a/u/i/aa*	ا	ا	ا
baa *b*	بـ	ـبـ	ب
taa *t*	تـ	ـتـ	ت
thaa *th*	ثـ	ـثـ	ث
jaa *j*	جـ	ـجـ	ج
Haa *H*	حـ	ـحـ	ح
khaa *kh*	خـ	ـخـ	خ
daal *d*	د	د	د
dhaal *dh*	ذ	ذ	ذ
raa *r*	ر	ر	ر
zaa *z*	ز	ز	ز
seen *s*	سـ	ـسـ	س
sheen *sh*	شـ	ـشـ	ش
Saad *S*	صـ	ـصـ	ص
Daad *D*	ضـ	ـضـ	ض
Taa *T*	طـ	ـطـ	ط
DHaa *DH*	ظـ	ـظـ	ظ
'ain *'*	عـ	ـعـ	ع/ـع
ghain *gh*	غـ	ـغـ	غ/ـغ
faa *f*	فـ	ـفـ	ف
qaaf *q*	قـ	ـقـ	ق
kaaf *k*	كـ	ـكـ	ك
laam *l*	لـ	ـلـ	ل

letter *sound*	*beginning*	*middle*	*end*
meem *m*	مـ	ـمـ	م
noon *n*	نـ	ـنـ	ن
haa *h*	هـ	ـهـ	ـه / ه
waaw *w/oo*	و	و	و
yaa *y/ee*	يـ	ـيـ	ي

ABBREVIATIONS

The following abbreviation are used in the dictionary:

adj	*adjective*
adv	*adverb*
coll	*colloquial*
fem	*feminine*
masc	*masculine*
n	*noun*
pl	*plural*
pron	*pronoun*
v	*verb*

ENGLISH–ARABIC DICTIONARY

Plurals of common words are given in transliteration after the singular, e.g. **abbey** *dair, adyira*.

Verbs are listed under the present tense, third person masculine ("he" form), e.g. *yaktub, yadrus*. Each verb is followed by a reference, e.g. **agree** (v, *III*). The roman numerals refer to the verb form (see page 188). Irregular verbs are also indicated, e.g. **add** (v, *I hollow*). Each type of irregular verb has tables for reference in the Appendix (pages 191–200).

You will also find a general introduction to Arabic verbs on page 188.

A

abbey	دير	dair, adyira
able	قدير	qadeer
above	أعلى	a'laa
absent	غائب	ghaa'ib
accent (n, speech)	لهجة	lahja, lahjaat
accept (v, I)	يقبل	yaqbal
accident	حادث	Haadith, Hawaadith
accomodation	إقامة	iqaama
account (n, bank)	حساب	Hisaab, Hisaabaat
accountant	محاسب	muHaasib, muHaasibeen
ache (n)	ألم	alam, aalaam
acidity	حموضة	HumooDa
across	بالعرض	bil'arD
activity	نشاط	nashaaT, anshiTa
add (v, I hollow)	يضيف	yuDeef
address (n, street)	عنوان	'unwaan, 'anaaween
adjust (v, II)	يعدل	yu'ad-dil
administration	إدارة	idaara
adolescent	مراهق	muraahiq, muraahiqeen
adult	راشد	raashid, raashideen

advanced (adj)	متقدم	*mutaqad-dim*
adventure	مغامرة	*mughaamara, mughaamaraat*
advertising (n)	إعلان	*i'laan*
advice (n)	نصيحة	*naSeeHa, naSaa'iH*
Afghan (adj)	أفغاني	*afghaaneyy, afghaan*
Afghanistan	أفغانستان	*afghaanistaan*
afraid	خائف	*khaa'if*
after (prep)	بعد	*ba'd*
afternoon (n)	بعد الظهر	*ba'd aDH-DHuhr*
again	مرة أخرى	*marra ukhra*
against	ضد	*Didd*
age (n)	سن	*sinn*
agency (n)	وكالة	*wikaala, wikaalaat*
agree (v, *III*)	يوافق	*yuwaafiq*
agriculture (n)	زراعة	*ziraa'a*
air (n)	هواء	*hawaa'*
air conditioning (n)	تكييف الهواء	*takyeef al-hawaa'*
airmail (n)	بريد جوي	*bareed jaw-weyy*
airplane	طائرة	*Taa'ira, Taa'iraat*
airport	مطار	*maTaar, maTaaraat*
alcohol	الكحول	*al-kuHool*
Algeria	الجزائر	*al-jazaa'ir*

Algerian	جزائري	*jazaa'ireyy, jazaa'irey-yeen*
alive	حي	*Hayy*
all	كل	*kull*
Allah	الله	*al-laah*
allergic	حساس	*Has-saas*
allow (v, I)	يسمح	*yasmaH*
almonds	لوز	*lawz*
almost	تقريبا	*taqreeban*
alone	منفرد	*munfarid*
also	أيضا	*aiDan*
altitude	ارتفاع	*irtifaa', irtifaa'aat*
always	دائما	*daa'iman*
ambassador	سفير	*safeer, sufaraa'*
amber	كهرمان	*kahramaan*
ambergris	عنبر	*'anbar*
ambulance	إسعاف	*is'aaf*
America	أمريكا	*amreeka*
American	أمريكي	*amreekeyy*
amicable	ودي	*wid-deyy*
amid	وسط	*wasT*
amount (n)	كمية	*kam-mey-ya, kam-mey-yaat*
amphitheater	مدرج	*mudar-raj*
ancestors	أسلاف	*aslaaf*
ancient	عتيق	*'ateeq*

angle (n)	زاوية	*zaawiya, zawaayaa*
angry	غاضب	*ghaaDib*
animal	حيوان	*Hayawaan, Hayawaanaat*
another	آخر	*aakhar*
answer (n)	إجابة	*ijaaba, ijaabaat*
antiques	تحف قديمة	*tuHaf qadeema*
antiseptic (adj)	مطهر	*muTah-hir*
anybody	أي شخص	*ayy shakhS*
anything	أي شيء	*ayy shai'*
anywhere	أي مكان	*ayy makaan*
apartment	شقة	*shiq-qa, shuqaq*
apologize (v, *VIII*)	يعتذر	*ya'tadhir*
appetizers	فواتح الشهية	*fawaatiH ash-shahey-ya*
apple	تفاحة	*tufaaHa, tufaaH*
appliance	جهاز	*jihaaz, ajhiza*
appointment	موعد	*maw'id, mawaa'eed*
apricot	مشمش	*mishmish*
Arab (adj)	عربي	*'arabeyy*
Arabic (language)	العربية	*al-'arabeyya*
architect	(مهندس) معماري	*mi'maareyy*
arm (n, anatomical)	ذراع	*dhiraa'*
around	حول	*Hawl*

14   ENGLISH–ARABIC

arrange (v, *II*)	يرتب	*yurat-tib*
arrival	وصول	*wuSool*
art	فن	*fann*
artery	شريان	*shiryaan, sharaayeen*
artichoke	خرشوف	*kharshoof* (coll.)
artificial	اصطناعي	*iSTinaa'eyy*
artist	فنان	*fannaan, fannaaneen*
ask (v, *I*)	يسأل	*yas'al*
asleep	نائم	*naa'im*
assist (v, *III*)	يعاون	*yu'aawin*
assortment	تشكيلة	*tashkeela*
asthma	ربو	*rabu*
astronomical	فلكي	*falakeyy*
athletic	رياضي	*riyaaDeyy*
attorney	محام	*muHaami, muHaami-yeen*
attractive	جذاب	*jadh-dhaab*
auction (n)	مزاد	*mazaad, mazaadaat*
aunt (maternal)	خالة	*khaala, khaalaat*
aunt (paternal)	عمة	*'am-ma, am-maat*
authentic	أصلي	*aSleyy*
author (n)	مؤلف	*mu'al-lif, mu'al-lifeen*

available	متوفر	*mutawaf-fir*
average	متوسط	*mutawas-siT*
azure	أزرق سماوي	*azraq samaaweyy*

B

Babylon	بابل	*baabil*
bachelor	أعزب	*a'zab, 'uzaab*
back (adj, rear)	خلفي	*khalfeyy*
back (n, anatomical)	ظهر	*DHahr, DHuhoor*
back (v, III; support)	يساند	*yusaanid*
backgammon	طاولة الزهر	*Tawlit az-zahr*
bad (rotten)	فاسد	*faasid*
bag (n)	حقيبة	*Haqeeba, Haqaa'ib*
baggage (n)	أمتعة	*amti'a*
Bahrain	البحرين	*al-baHrayn*
Bahraini	بحريني	*baHrayneyy*
bakery	مخبز	*makhbaz, makhaabiz*
balance (n, scales)	ميزان	*meezaan*
balcony	شرفة	*shurfa, shurfaat*
bald	أصلع	*aSla'*
ball (n)	كرة	*kura, kuraat*
bamboo (n)	خيزران	*khaizaraan*
banana	موزة	*mawza, mawz*

bangle	خلخال	*khal-khaal, khalaa-kheel*
barber	حلاق	*Hal-laaq, Hal-laaqeen*
bargain (n)	صفقة	*Safqa, Safqaat*
base (n, foundation)	أساس	*asaas*
basil	ريحان	*reeHaan*
basket	سلة	*sal-la*
bathroom	حمام	*Ham-maam*
bay	شرم	*sharm*
bay leaves	ورق الغار	*waraq al-ghaar*
beach	شاطئ	*shaaTi', shawaaTi'*
beans (fava)	فول	*fool*
beans (green)	فاصوليا	*faSolya*
beans (runner)	لوبيا	*lubya*
beard	لحية	*liHya, liHaa*
beat (n, tempo, music)	إيقاع	*eeqaa'*
beat (v, I; hit)	يضرب	*yaDrib*
beaten (adj, whisked)	مخفوق	*makhfooq*
beautiful	جميل	*jameel*
because	لأن	*la'ann*
become	يصبح	*yuSbiH*
bed	سرير	*sareer, asir-ra*
Bedouin	بدوي	*badaweyy*
bedroom	غرفة نوم	*ghurfat nawm*
bee	نحلة	*naHla, naHl*

beech (wood)	خشب الزان	*khashab az-zaan*
beef	لحم بقري	*laHm baqareyy*
beer	بيرة	*beera*
before	قبل	*qabl*
begin (v, I)	يبدأ	*yabda'*
behind	خلف	*khalf*
belief	إيمان	*eemaan*
believe (v, II)	يصدق	*yuSad-diq*
below	أسفل	*asfal*
bend (n, contour)	انحناء	*inHinaa'*
benefit (n)	فائدة	*faa'ida, fawaa'id*
Berber	بربر	*barbar*
beside	بجانب	*bijaanib*
best (adj & n)	أحسن	*aHsan*
bet (n)	رهان	*rahaan, rahaanaat*
Bethlehem	بيت لحم	*bait laHm*
better (adj & n)	أفضل	*afDal*
between	بين	*bain*
beyond	ما وراء	*maa waraa'*
Bible	انجيل	*injeel*
bicycle	دراجة	*dar-raaja, dar-raajaat*
big	كبير	*kabeer*
bilingual	بلغتين	*bilughatain*
bird	طائر	*Taa'ir, Tiyoor*
birth (n)	ولادة	*wilaada, wilaadaat*

birthday	عيد ميلاد	'eed milaad
black (color)	أسود	aswad
black coffee (no sugar)	قهوة سادة	qahwa saada
bladder	مثانة	mathaana
blank	فارغ	faarigh
blanket	بطانية	baT-Taney-ya, baTaaTeen
bleed (v, I)	ينزف	yanzif
blend (n, mix)	خليط	khaleeT
blind (adj, without sight)	أعمى	a'maa
blonde (adj)	أشقر	ashqar
blood (n)	دم	dam
blood type/group	فصيلة الدم	faSeelat ad-dam
blood test	فحص دم	faHS dam
blood transfusion	نقل دم	naql dam
blouse	بلوزة	bilooza
blue	أزرق	azraq
boat	مركب	markib, maraakib
body	جسم	jism, ajsaam
boil (v, I defective; heat)	يغلي	yaghlee
bone	عظمة	'aDHma, 'iDHaam
book (n, novel, etc.)	كتاب	kitaab, kutub
book (v, I; reserve)	يحجز	yaHjiz
bookshop	مكتبة	maktaba, maktabaat
boring (adj, tedious)	ممل	mumill

bottle (n, glass container)	زجاجة	*zujaaja, zujaajaat*
box (n)	علبة	*'ulba, 'ulab*
boy	ولد	*walad, awlaad*
bracelet	سوار	*siwaar*
brain	مخ	*mukh*
brakes	مكابح	*makaabiH*
brass	نحاس أصفر	*naHaas aSfar*
bread	خبز	*khubz*
break (n, respite)	استراحة	*istiraaHa*
break (v, I; smash)	يكسر	*yaksir*
breakdown (itemization)	بيان مفصل	*bayaan mufaS-Sal*
breakdown (malfunction)	تعطل	*Ta'aT-Tul*
breakdown (nervous)	انهيار عصبي	*inhiyaar 'aSabeyy*
breakfast	فطور	*fuToor*
breast	صدر	*Sadr, Sudoor*
breed (n)	سلالة	*sulaala, sulaalaat*
breed (v, II defective)	يربي	*yurab-bee*
bride	عروسة	*'aroosa, 'araa'is*
bridegroom	عريس	*'arees, 'irsaan*
bridge (n)	جسر	*jisr, jusoor*
Britain	بريطانيا	*biriTaanya*
British (adj)	بريطاني	*biriTaaneyy, biriTaaney-yeen*
broker	سمسار	*simsaar, samaasira*
brother	أخ	*akh, ukhwa*

brown	بني	*bun-neyy*
budget (adj, cheap)	اقتصادي	*iqtiSaadeyy*
budget (n, fiscal framework)	ميزانية	*meezaney-ya*
buffalo	جاموسة	*jaamoosa, jaamoos*
building	بناء	*binaa', abneya*
bureau de change	مكتب صراف	*maktab Sar-raaf*
bureaucracy	بيروقراطية	*beeroqraTey-ya*
burglary	سرقة	*sariqa, sariqaat*
burn (v, *I*)	يحرق	*yaHriq*
burst (v, *VII*)	ينفجر	*yan-fajir*
bus	باص	*baaS, baaSaat*
busy (adj)	مشغول	*mash-ghool*
butcher (n)	جزار	*jaz-zaar, jaz-zaareen*
butter	زبد	*zubd*
button (n)	زر	*zirr*
buy (v, *VIII defective*)	يشتري	*yashtaree*

C

cab (n)	تاكسي	*taksee*
cabin (n)	كابينة	*kabeena, kabaa'in*
cable (n)	سلك	*silk, aslaak*
cactus	صبار	*Sab-baar*
Cairo	القاهرة	*al-qaahira*
calculate (v, *I*)	يحسب	*yaHsib*

caliph	خليفة	*khaleefa, kholafaa'*
call (n, a phonecall)	مكالمة	*mukaalama, mukaalamaat*
call (v, VIII; phone)	يتصل	*yat-taSil*
call (v, III defective; summon)	ينادي	*yunaadee*
calligraphy	فن الخط	*fann al-khaTT*
calm (adj)	ساكن	*saakin*
camel	جمل	*jamal, jimaal*
camping trip (n)	التخييم	*at-takhyeem*
canal (n, channel)	قناة	*qanaah, qanawaat*
cancellation	إلغاء	*ilghaa'*
candle	شمعة	*sham'a, shimoo'*
candy	حلوى	*Halwaa*
canvas	خيش	*khuish*
capital (city)	عاصمة	*'aaSima, 'awaaSim*
car	سيارة	*say-yaara, say-yaaraat*
carafe	دورق	*dawraq, dawaariq*
card	بطاقة	*biTaaqa, biTaaqaat*
cardamom	حبهان	*Hab-bahaan*
care (n)	عناية	*'inaaya*
carelessness (n)	إهمال	*ihmaal*
carnation	قرنفل	*qaranful*
carnelian	عقيق أحمر	*'aqeeq aHmar*
carpenter	نجار	*naj-jaar, naj-jaareen*

carpet (n)	سجادة	*sij-jaada, sij-jaad*
carrot	جزر	*jazar*
carry (v, I)	يحمل	*yaHmil*
Casablanca	الدار البيضاء	*ad-daar al-bayDaa'*
case (n, court)	قضية	*qaDey-ya*
case (n, instance)	حالة	*Haala*
case (n, pillow)	كيس وسادة	*kees wisaada*
castle	قلعة	*qal'a, qilaa'*
cat	قطة	*qiT-Ta, qiTaT*
catacomb	سرداب	*sirdaab, saraadeeb*
catch (v I; hold)	يمسك	*yamsik*
catch (v VIII hollow; hunt)	يصطاد	*yaSTaad*
cause (n, reason)	سبب	*sabab, asbaab*
caution (n, prudence)	احتراس	*iHtiraas*
caution (n, warning)	تحذير	*taHdheer*
cave (n)	كهف	*kahf, kuhoof*
cavity	تجويف	*tajweef*
cedar (n)	شجرة الأرز	*shajarat al-arz*
ceiling	سقف	*saqf*
celebration	احتفال	*iHtifaal, iHtifaalaat*
celery	كرفس	*karafs*
central (adj, main)	مركزي	*markazeyy*
central (adj, middle)	متوسط	*muTawas-siT*
cereal (breakfast)	حبوب الفطور	*Huboob al-fuToor*
certainty	يقين	*yaqeen*

chair	كرسي	*kursee, karaasee*
chance	صدفة	*Sudfa*
change (n, alteration)	تغيير	*taghyeer, taghyeeraat*
change (n, coins)	فكة	*fak-ka*
change (v II, money, etc.)	يغير	*yughay-yir*
charge (n, accusation)	تهمة	*tuhma*
charge (n, fee)	أجر	*ajr, ujoor*
charge (v I, fill up)	يشحن	*yash-Hin*
charge card	بطاقة حساب	*biTaaqat Hisaab*
charity (n, donation)	صدقة	*Sadaqa, Sadaqaat*
charity (n, organization)	منظمة خيرية	*munaDH-DHama khairey-ya*
cheap	رخيص	*rakheeS*
cheat (v, I doubled)	يغش	*yaghishsh*
check (adj, pattern)	مربعات	*murab-ba'aat*
check (n, bill)	فاتورة	*fatoora, fawaateer*
cheese	جبنة	*jubna*
chemistry	كيمياء	*keemyaa'*
cherries	كرز	*karz*
chicken	دجاج	*dajaaj*
chickpeas	حمص	*Hum-muS*
child	طفل	*Tifl, aTfaal*
choice	اختيار	*ikhtiyaar*
Christian	مسيحي	*maseeHeyy, maseeHey-yeen*

Christianity	المسيحية	al-maseeHey-ya
chronic	مزمن	muzmin
church	كنيسة	kaneesa, kanaa'is
circle (n)	دائرة	daa'ira, dawaa'ir
circumcision	ختان	khitaan
citadel	قلعة	qal'a, qilaa'
city	مدينة	madeena, mudun
civilization	حضارة	HaDaara, HaDaaraat
clean (adj)	نظيف	naDHeef
clear (adj, unambiguous)	واضح	waaDiH
clear (adj, unclouded)	صافي	Saafi
client	زبون	zuboon, zabaa'in
climb (n)	تسلق	tasal-luq
climb (v, V)	يتسلق	yatasal-laq
close (adv, near)	قريب	qareeb
closed	مغلق	mughlaq
closet	خزانة ملابس	khazaanat malaabis
clothes	ملابس	malaabis
coach (n, bus)	باص	baaS, baaSaat
coach (n, trainer)	مدرب	mudar-rib, mudar-ribeen
coast (n, shore)	ساحل	saaHil, sawaaHil
coffee (beans)	بن	bunn
coffee (beverage)	قهوة	qahwa

coffee cup reader	قارئة الفنجان	*qaari'at al-finjaan*
cold (adj)	بارد	*baarid*
college	كلية	*kul-ley-ya, kul-ley-yaat*
colloquial language	العامية	*al-'aamey-ya*
color (n)	لون	*lawn, alwaan*
come (v, I defective)	يأتي	*ya'tee*
comfortable	مريح	*mureeH*
commercial district	حي تجاري	*Hayy tijaareyy*
commission (n, percentage fee)	عمولة	*'umoola, 'umoolaat*
common (adj, familiar)	مألوف	*ma'loof*
companion	رفيق	*rafeeq, rifaaq*
company (n, business)	شركة	*sharika, sharikaat*
company (n, guests)	ضيوف	*Duyoof*
compensation	تعويض	*ta'weeD*
complain (v, I defective)	يشكو	*yashkoo*
complement (v, II) (v, make whole)	يكمل	*yukam-mil*
compliment (v, I)	يمدح	*yamdaH*
complimentary	مجاني	*maj-jaaneyy*
compromise (n)	حل وسط	*Hall wasaT*
compulsory	اجباري	*ijbaari*
concerned (worried)	قلق	*qaliq*
concert (n)	حفلة موسيقية	*Hafla museeqey-ya*
concussion	ارتجاج	*irtijaaj*

condition (n, state)	حالة	Haala
condition (n, stipulation)	شرط	sharT, shurooT
condom	عازل طبي	'aazil Tib-beyy, 'awaazil Tib-bey-ya
confirm (v, II)	يؤكد	yu'ak-kid
connect (v, IV)	يوصل	yawSil
consent (n)	تراض	taraaDi
constant	دائم	daa'im
constipation	إمساك	imsaak
construct (v, II)	يشيد	yushay-yid
consulate	قنصلية	qunSuley-ya, qunSuley-yaat
consultant	استشاري	istishaareyy
contagious	معد	mu'di
contradictory	متناقض	mutanaaqiD
convenient	مناسب	munaasib
cook (n, chef)	طباخ	Tab-baakh, Tab-baakheen
cook (v, I)	يطبخ	yaTbukh
Copt (n)	قبطي	qibTeyy, aqbaaT
coral	شعاب مرجانية	shi'aab mar jaaney-ya
corner (n)	ركن	rukn, arkaan
cost (n)	ثمن	thaman
cotton (n)	قطن	quTn
cough (n)	سعال	su'aal

count (v, *I doubled*; compute) يعد *ya'idd*

country (n, state) دولة *dawla*

countryside ريف *reef*

couple اثنين *ithnain*

cousin (daughter of maternal aunt) بنت خالة *bint khaala, banaat khaala*

cousin (daughter of maternal uncle) بنت خال *bint khaal, banaat khaal*

cousin (daughter of paternal aunt) بنت عمة *bint 'amma, banaat 'amma*

cousin (daughter of paternal uncle) بنت عم *bint 'amm, banaat 'amm*

cousin (son of maternal aunt) ابن خالة *ibn khaala, abnaa' khaala*

cousin (son of maternal uncle) ابن خال *ibn khaal, abnaa' khaal*

cousin (son of paternal aunt) ابن عمة *ibn 'amma, abnaa' 'amma*

cousin (son of paternal uncle) ابن عم *ibn 'amm, abnaa' 'amm*

cover (n, lid) غطاء *ghaTaa', aghTey-ya*

cover (v, *II*) يغطي *yughaTTi'*

coverage (n, insurance) تأمين *ta'meen*

cow بقرة *baqara, baqar*

craftsmanship حرفية *Hirafey-ya*

crash (n) تصادم *taSaadum*

crazy مخبول *makhbool*

creativity	ابتكار	*ibtikaar*
credit (n)	ضمان	*Damaan*
crescent	هلال	*hilaal*
crime	جريمة	*jareema, jaraa'im*
criminal (n)	مجرم	*mujrim, mujrimeen*
critical (adj, dangerous)	خطير	*khaTeer*
crocodile	تمساح	*timsaaH, tamaaseeH*
crook	نصاب	*naS-Saab, naS-Saabeen*
cross (adj, angry)	غضبان	*ghaDbaan*
cross (n, crucifix)	صليب	*Saleeb*
cross (v II, interbreed)	يهجن	*yahaj-jin*
cross (v I, road, etc.)	يعبر	*ya'bur*
cruise (n)	جولة بحرية	*jawla baHrey-ya*
crushed (adj, powdered)	مسحوق	*masHooq*
cry (v I defective; weep)	يبكي	*yabkee*
cry (v I; yell)	يصرخ	*yaSrukh*
cucumber	خيار	*khiyaar*
cul-de-sac	طريق مسدود	*Tareeq masdood*
cultured (erudite)	مثقف	*muthaq-qaf, muthaq-qafeen*
cup (n, for drinks)	فنجان	*finjaan, fanajeen*
cup (n, trophy)	كأس	*ka's, ku'oos*
cure (n, treatment)	علاج	*'ilaaj*

currency	عملة	*'umla, 'umlaat*
current (n, electric)	تيار كهربائي	*tay-yaar kahrubaa'eyy*
current (n, water)	تيار مائي	*tay-yaar maa'eyy*
current account	حساب جار	*Hisaab jaari*
current affairs	شؤون الساعة	*shu'oon as-saa'a*
curse (n, evil spell)	لعنة	*la'na*
curse (v, I; abuse verbally)	يشتم	*yashtim*
curtain	ستار	*sitaar*
customs (n, import duties)	جمارك	*jamaarik*
customs (n, traditions)	تقاليد	*taqaaleed*
cut (v, I; tear)	يقطع	*yaqTa'*
cycling	ركوب الدراجات	*rukoob ad-dar-raajaat*

D

dagger	خنجر	*khanjar, khanaajir*
daily	يومي	*yawmeyy*
dairy products	منتجات الألبان	*muntajaat al-albaan*
dam	سد	*sadd, sudood*
damage (n)	تلف	*talaf*
Damascus	دمشق	*dimashq*
dance (v, I)	يرقص	*yarquS*

dangerous	خطر	*khaTir*
dark (unlit)	مظلم	*muDHlim*
date (appointment)	موعد	*maw'id, mawaa'eed*
date (day)	تاريخ	*taareekh, tawaareekh*
date (fruit)	بلحة	*balaHa, balaH*
date (tree)	نخلة	*nakhla, nakhlaat*
daughter	ابنة	*ibna, banaat*
dawn (n)	فجر	*fajr*
day	يوم	*yawm, ayaam*
deadly	مميت	*mumeet*
deaf	أصم	*aSamm*
decide (v, *II*)	يقرر	*yaqar-rir*
deduct (v, *I*)	يخصم	*yakhSim*
deep (adj)	عميق	*'ameeq*
deer	غزال	*ghazaal*
degree (extent)	درجة	*daraja, darajaat*
degree (university certificate)	شهادة جامعية	*shihaada jaame'ey-ya*
delicate	رقيق	*raqeeq*
deliver (v, *II*)	يوصل	*yuwaS-Sil*
dense	كثيف	*katheef*
dentist	طبيب أسنان	*Tabeeb asnaan*
dentures	طقم أسنان	*Taqm asnaan*
departure	رحيل	*raHeel*

deport (v, I)	يطرد	yaTrud
deposit	يودع	yudi'
(v, IV; place securely)		
dervish	درويش	darweesh,
		daraaweesh
descendant	سليل	saleel
describe (v, I assimilated)	يصف	yaSif
desert (n)	صحراء	SaHraa'
design (v, II)	يصمم	yuSam-mim
dessert	طبق الحلو	Tabaq al-Hilw
destination	وجهة	wijha, wijhaat
details	تفاصيل	tafaaSeel
detergent	منظف	munaDH-DHif,
		munaDH-DHifaat
devil	شيطان	shayTaan,
		shayaaTeen
diabetes	مرض السكر	maraD as-suk-kar
diagnosis	تشخيص	tash-kheeS
dial (v, I)	يطلب بالتليفون	yaTlub bit-tilifoon
dialect	لهجة	lahja, lahjaat
dial tone	حرارة (تليفون)	Haraara
diamonds	ماس	maas
diaper	حفاضة	Haf-faaDa
diarrhea	إسهال	is-haal
dictionary	قاموس	qaamoos,
		qawaamees

diet	نظام تغذية	*niDHaam tagh-dheya*
difference	فرق	*farq, furooq*
difficult	صعب	*Sa'b*
dinner	عشاء	*'ashaa'*
direct (adj, non-stop)	مباشر	*mubaashir*
direct (v, *IV*; a movie, etc.)	يخرج	*yukhrij*
direct (v, *I doubled*; give directions)	يدل	*yadull*
director (n, executive)	مدير	*mudeer*
dirty (adj)	قذر	*qadhir*
disability	عجز	*'ajz*
disabled (n)	معاق	*mu'aaq*
discount (n)	خصم	*khaSm, khuSumaat*
disease	مرض	*maraD, amraaD*
dish (n)	طبق	*Tabaq, aTbaaq*
dishwasher	غسالة أطباق	*ghas-saalat aTbaaq*
disinfect (v, *II*)	يطهر	*yuTah-hir*
dissolve (v, *I hollow*)	يذوب	*yudhoob*
distance (n)	مسافة	*masaafa*
divide (v, *II*)	يقسم	*yuqas-sim*
diving (n, scuba)	غوص	*ghawS*
divorce (n)	طلاق	*Talaaq*
dog	كلب	*kalb, kilaab*
doll	دمية	*dumya, dumyaat*
dolphin	درفيل	*darfeel, daraafeel*

dome	قبة	qub-ba, qibaab
donkey	حمار	Himaar, Hameer
door	باب	baab, abwaab
doorbell	جرس الباب	jaras al-baab
dosage	جرعة	jur'a, jur'aat
double (adj)	مزدوج	muzdawaj
doubt (n)	شك	shakk
dough	عجين	'ajeen
down (n, feathers)	زغب	zaghab
down payment	مقدم	muqad-dam
downriver	مع مجرى النهر	ma' majraa an-nahr
down(wards)	إلى أسفل	ila asfal
dozen	دستة	dasta
draw (v, I; attract)	يجذب	yajdhub
draw (v, I; illustrate)	يرسم	yarsim
draw (v, I doubled; pull behind)	يجر	yajurr
dream (n)	حلم	Hilm, aHlaam
dream (v, I)	يحلم	yaHlam
dress (n, clothing item)	فستان	fustaan, fasaateen
dressing (n, salad flavoring)	توابل السلطة	tawaabil as-salaTa
drink (n)	مشروب	mashroob, mashroobaat
drink (v, I)	يشرب	yashrib

driver	سائق	saa'iq, saa'iqeen
drown (v, I)	يغرق	yaghriq
drug (medication)	دواء	dawaa', adweya
drug (narcotic)	مخدر	mukhad-dir, mukhad-diraat
drugstore	صيدلية	Saydaley-ya, Saydaley-yaat
dry (adj)	جاف	jaaf
duck (n)	بطة	baT-Ta, baTT
during (prep)	خلال	khilaal
dust (n)	تراب	turaab
duty (n, obligation)	واجب	waajib, waajibaat
duty (n, tax)	ضريبة	Dareeba, Daraa'ib
dye (v, I)	يصبغ	yaSbigh
dynasty (n)	أسرة حاكمة	usra Haakima

E

each	كل	kull
eagle	نسر	nisr, nisoor
ear	أذن	udhun, aadhaan
early	مبكر	mubak-kir
Earth (planet)	الكرة الأرضية	al-kura l-arDey-ya
east (n)	شرق	sharq
Easter	عيد الفصح	eed al-fiSH
eastern	شرقي	sharqeyy

eat (v, I)	يأكل	*ya'kul*
economic	اقتصادي	*iqtiSaadeyy*
edge	حد	*Hadd, Hudood*
education	تعليم	*ta'leem*
effective	فعال	*fa'aal*
effort	جهد	*juhd, juhood*
egg	بيضة	*baiDa, baiD*
eggplant	باذنجان	*baadhinjaan*
Egypt	مصر	*miSr*
Egyptian	مصري	*misreyy, miSrey-yeen*
Egyptology	علم المصريات	*'ilm al-miSrey-yaat*
elbow	كوع	*koo', akwaa'*
elder (n)	الأكبر	*al-akbar*
elderly (adj)	مسن	*musinn, musin-neen*
electricity	كهرباء	*kahrabaa'*
elementary (basic)	أساسي	*asaaseyy*
elephant	فيل	*feel, afyaal*
elevator	مصعد	*miS'ad, maSaa'id*
else	آخر	*aakhar*
embalming (n)	تحنيط	*taHneeT*
embassy	سفارة	*sifaara, sifaaraat*
embroidered	مطرز	*moTar-raz*
emerald (n)	زمرد	*zumur-rud*
emergency (n)	طوارئ	*Tawaari'*

emir	أمير	*ameer, umaraa'*
Emirates (United Arab)	الإمارات	*al-imaaraat*
employee	موظف	*muwaDH-DHaf,*
		muwaDH-DHafeen
empty	فارغ	*faarigh*
end (n)	نهاية	*nihaaya*
energetic	نشيط	*nasheeT*
engagement	ارتباط	*irtibaaT,*
(n, appointment)		*irtibaaTaat*
engagement	خطوبة	*khuTooba*
(n, for marriage)		
engine	محرك	*muHar-rik,*
		muHar-rikaat
engineer	مهندس	*muhandis,*
		muhandiseen
England	انجلترا	*ingeltera*
English (language)	اللغة الانجليزية	*al-lugha*
		al-ingeleezey-ya
English (person)	انجليزي	*ingeleezeyy,*
		ingeleez
engraved (adj)	منقوش	*manqoosh*
enjoy (v, X)	يستمتع	*yastamti'*
enough	كفاية	*kifaaya*
enter (v, I)	يدخل	*yadkhol*
entertainment	تسلية	*tasliya*
entrance	مدخل	*madkhal,*
		madaakhil

envelope	مظروف	*maDHroof,* *maDHaareef*
environment	بيئة	*bee'a*
epilepsy (n)	صرع	*Sara'*
equal (adj)	مساو	*musawi*
equestrian (adj)	خاص بالفروسية	*khaaS bil-furoosey-ya*
error	خطأ	*khaTa', akhTaa'*
escape (v, I)	يهرب	*yahrab*
essential	ضروري	*Darooreyy*
estimate (n)	تقدير	*taqdeer*
estimate (v, II)	يقدر	*yuqad-dir*
Euphrates	الفرات	*al-furaat*
Euro	اليورو	*al-yooroo*
Europe	أوروبا	*orob-baa*
European	أوروبي	*orob-beyy,* *orob-bey-yeen*
even (adj, leveled)	متساو	*mutasaawi*
evening	مساء	*masaa'*
ever (adv)	أبدا	*abadan*
every	كل	*kull*
exact	مضبوط	*maDbooT*
examination (n, medical)	فحص	*faHS, fuHooSaat*
examination (n, school)	امتحان	*imtiHaan,* *imtiHaanaat*
example	مثال	*mithaal, amthila*

excavation	تنقيب	*tanqeeb*
exceed (v, *VI*)	يتجاوز	*yatajaawaz*
excellence	امتياز	*imtiyaaz*
except	ما عدا	*maa 'adaa*
exchange (n)	مبادلة	*mubaadala*
exchange (v, *III*)	يبادل	*yubaadil*
excursion	جولة	*jawla, jawlaat*
excuse (n)	عذر	*'udhr, a'dhaar*
exempt	معفي	*ma'fi*
exercise (n)	تمرين	*tamreen, tamreenaat*
exhaust (n, fumes)	عادم	*'aadim*
exhausted	مرهق	*murhaq*
exhibition	معرض	*mua'riD, ma'aariD*
exit (n)	مخرج	*makhraj, makhaarij*
expect (v, *V*)	يتوقع	*yatawaq-qa'*
expenses	مصاريف	*maSaareef*
expensive	غال	*ghali*
experience (n)	خبرة	*khibra, khibraat*
expiration date	تاريخ انتهاء الصلاحية	*tareekh intihaa' aS-SalaaHiya*
explain (v, *I*)	يشرح	*yashraH*
explore (v, *X*)	يستكشف	*yastakshif*
expression (phrase)	تعبير	*ta'beer, ta'beeraat*
exterior	خارجي	*khaarijeyy*

extinguish (v, *IV*)	يطفئ	*yuTfi'*
extra	إضافي	*iDaafeyy*
extraction (n, tooth, etc.)	خلع	*khal'*
eye (n, anatomical)	عين	*'ain, 'uyoon*
eyebrow	حاجب	*Haajib, Hawaajib*
eyelash	رمش	*rimsh, rumoosh*
eyesight	بصر	*baSar*

F

fabric	قماش	*qumaash, aqmisha*
face (n, anatomy)	وجه	*wajh, wujooh*
fact	حقيقة	*Haqeeqa, Haqaa'iq*
factory	مصنع	*maSna', maSaani'*
faint (pass out)	يغمى عليه	*yughma 'alaih*
fair (just)	عادل	*'aadil*
faith	إيمان	*'eeman*
faithful (adj)	وفي	*wafeyy*
fake (adj)	مزيف	*muzayyaf*
falcon	صقر	*Saqr, Suqoor*
fall (n, season)	الخريف	*al-khareef*
fall (v, *I*; tumble)	يسقط	*yasquT*
family	أسرة	*usra, usarr*
famous	مشهور	*mash-hoor*
fan (n, cooling)	مروحة	*marwaHa, maraawiH*

far	بعيد	ba'eed
fare	أجرة	ujra
farm (n)	مزرعة	mazra'a, mazaari'
fashion	موضة	moDa
fast (adj, speedy)	سريع	saree'
fast (n)	صوم	Sawm
fast (v, I hollow)	يصوم	yaSoom
fat (n)	دهن	duhn
fatal	مميت	mumeet
father (n)	أب	ab
father-in-law	حمو	Hamw
faucet	حنفية	Hanafey-ya, Hanafey-yaat
fault (n)	خلل	khalal
fear (n)	خوف	khawf
fear (v, I hollow)	يخاف من	yakhaaf min
feast (n)	عيد	'eed, a'yaad
feed (v, IV)	يطعم	yuT'im
feel (v, I)	يشعر	yash'ur
female	أنثى	untha
ferry (n)	معدية	mi'ad-dey-ya
festival	مهرجان	mahrajaan
fever	حمى	Hum-maa
few (adj)	قليل	qaleel
fez	طربوش	Tarboosh
fiancé (male)	خطيب	khaTeeb

fiancée (female)	خطيبة	*khaTeeba*
fig	تينة	*teena, teen*
fight (v, *III*)	يقاتل	*yuqaatil*
fill (v, *I*)	يملأ	*yamla'*
filly	مهرة	*muhra*
final	نهائي	*nihaa'i*
find (v, *I assimilated*)	يجد	*yajid*
fine (n)	غرامة	*gharaama, gharaamaat*
finger	إصبع	*iSba', aSaabi'*
finish (v, *IV defective*)	ينهي	*yunhee*
fire (n, flame)	نار	*naar*
fire (v, *I;* terminate employment)	يفصل	*yafSil*
first	أول	*aw-wal*
fish (n)	سمك	*samak*
fish (v, *VIII hollow*)	يصطاد سمك	*yaSTaaD samak*
fitting (adj, suitable)	مناسب	*munaasib*
fitting (n, trying on)	قياس	*qiyaas*
fix (v, *IV*)	يصلح	*yuSliH*
flat (adj, opp. bumpy)	مسطح	*musaT-TaH*
flavor	مذاق	*madhaaq*
flight (n, air journey)	رحلة طيران	*riHlat Tayaraan*
floor (n)	أرضية	*arDey-ya*
florist	محل ورد	*maHall ward*
flour	دقيق	*daqeeq*

flower (n, rose, etc.)	وردة	*warda, ward*
flush (n)	سيفون	*seefon*
fly (n, insect)	ذبابة	*dhobaaba, dhobaab*
fly (n, zipper)	سوستة	*sosta, sosat*
fly (v, I hollow)	يطير	*yaTeer*
fog	ضباب	*Dabaab*
follow (v, I)	يتبع	*yatba'*
food	أكل	*akl*
foot	قدم	*qadam, aqdaam*
forbidden	ممنوع	*mamnoo'*
foreigner	أجنبي	*ajnabee*
forget (v, I defective)	ينسى	*yansa*
fork	شوكة	*shawka, shuwak*
formal (adj)	رسمي	*rasmee*
fortress	قلعة	*qal'a, qilaa'*
forward (adj)	أمامي	*amaameyy*
fountain	نافورة	*nafoora, nafooraat*
fracture (n)	كسر	*kasr*
fragile	هش	*hash-sh*
frank (honest)	صريح	*SareeH*
free (adj, gratis)	مجاني	*maj-jaaneyy*
fresh	طازج	*Taazij*
fridge	ثلاجة	*thal-laaja, thal-laajaat*
friend	صديق	*Sadeeq, aSdiqaa'*

frozen (adj)	مجمد	*mujam-mad*
fruit	فاكهة	*faakiha, fawaakih*
fry (v, *I defective*)	يقلي	*yaqlee*
fuel (n)	وقود	*waqood*
full	كامل	*kaamil*
funny (humorous)	مضحك	*muD-Hik*
funny (peculiar)	غريب	*ghareeb*
future (n)	مستقبل	*mustaqbal*

G

gallant	شهم	*shahm*
gallery (n, exhibition)	معرض	*ma'raD, ma'aariD*
gallon	جالون	*galoon*
gambling	قمار	*qumaar*
garden	حديقة	*Hadeeqa, Hadaa'iq*
garlic	ثوم	*thawm*
gas (n, petrol)	بنزين	*banzeen*
gastric	معوي	*ma'aweyy*
gate	بوابة	*baw-waaba, baw-waabaat*
gazelle	غزال	*ghazaal, ghuzlaan*
gem	جوهرة	*jawhara, jawaahir*
generous	كريم	*kareem*
genuine	أصلي	*aSleyy*
germs	جراثيم	*jaraatheem*

gift	هدية	hadey-ya, hadaaya
ginger (n, herb)	جنزبيل	ganzabeel
girl	بنت	bint, banaat
give (v, IV defective)	يعطي	yu'Tee
gland	غدة	ghud-da, ghud-dad
glass (n, material)	زجاج	zujaaj
glass (n, tumbler, etc.)	كوب	koob, akwaab
glasses	نظارة	naDH-DHaara
go (v, I)	يذهب	yadh-hab
goat	عنزة	'anza, anzaat
God	الله	al-laah
gold (n)	ذهب	dhahab
good	حسن	Hasan
gossip (v, quadriteral)	يدردش	yudardish
grace (n, elegance)	رشاقة	rashaaqa
graduate (adj)	خريج	khir-reej
grandchild	حفيد	Hafeed, aHfaad
grandfather	جد	jidd
grape	عنبة	'inaba, 'inab
gratitude (adj)	امتنان	imtinaan
gratuity	إكرامية	ikraamey-ya, ikraamey-yaat
great (adj, marvelous)	عظيم	'aDHeem
greeting (n)	تحية	taHey-ya, taHey-yaat
grocer	بقال	baq-qaal

group (n)	مجموعة	*majmoo'a,*
		majmoo'aat
grow (v, *I defective*)	ينمو	*yanmoo*
guard (n)	حارس	*Haaris, Hor-ras*
guardian	وصي	*waSeyy*
guava	جوافة	*jawaafa*
guest (n)	ضيف	*Daif, Duyoof*
guidebook	دليل	*daleel*
gulf	خليج	*khaleej*
gynecology	أمراض نساء	*amraaD nisaa'*

H

habitat	موطن	*mawTin*
haggle (v, *III*)	يساوم	*yusaawim*
hair	شعر	*sha'r*
hairdresser	كوافير	*kewafeer*
half	نصف	*niSf, anSaaf*
hall	بهو	*bahw*
hand (n, anatomy)	يد	*yad, ayaadi*
handbag	حقيبة يد	*Haqeebat yad*
handkerchief	منديل	*mindeel*
handsome	وسيم	*waseem*
happen (v, *I*)	يحدث	*yaHduth*
happy	سعيد	*sa'eed*
harass	يضايق	*yuDaayiq*

harbor	ميناء	*meena', mawaani'*
harm (n)	ضرر	*Darar*
hat	قبعة	*quba'a*
hate (v, I)	يكره	*yakrah*
have	يملك	*yamluk*
hawk	صقر	*Saqr, Suqoor*
hazard	خطر	*khaTar*
head (n, anatomy)	رأس	*ra's, ru'oos*
head (v, move towards)	يتجه	*yat-tajih*
headache	صداع	*Sodaa'*
headlights	ضوء عال	*Daw' 'aali*
heal (mend)	يلتئم	*yalta'im*
health	صحة	*SiH-Ha*
heart	قلب	*qalb, quloob*
heat (n)	سخونة	*sukhoona*
heater	مدفأة	*midfa'a*
heavy	ثقيل	*thaqeel*
help (n)	مساعدة	*musaa'ida*
help (v, III)	يساعد	*yusaa'id*
henna	حناء	*Henaa'*
hepatitis	صفراء	*Safraa'*
herb	عشب	*'ushb, a'shaab*
here	هنا	*huna*
hereditary	وراثي	*wiraathy*
hieroglyphic	هيروغليفي	*heeroghleefee*
high (tall)	عال	*aali*

hill	تل	*tall, tilaal*
hire (v, *II*)	يؤجر	*yu'aj-jir*
history	تاريخ	*tareekh*
hobby	هواية	*huwaaya, huwayaat*
hold (v, *I*; grip)	يمسك	*yamsik*
hole	ثقب	*thuqb, thuqoob*
holiday (n)	عطلة	*uTla, uTlaat*
holy	مقدس	*muqad-das*
home (dwelling)	بيت	*bait, buyoot*
honey	عسل	*'asal*
hoof	حافر	*Haafir, Hawaafir*
hookah	شيشة	*sheesha*
hope (v, *I*)	يأمل	*ya'mal*
hornet	دبور	*dab-boor, dabaabeer*
horse	حصان	*HiSaan, aHSina*
hospital	مستشفى	*mustashfa*
hospitality	كرم الضيافة	*karam aD-Diyaafa*
hot	حار	*Harr*
hotel	فندق	*funduq, fanaadiq*
hotel lobby	صالة الفندق	*Saalat al-funduq*
hour	ساعة	*saa'a, sa'aat*
house	دار	*daar, diyaar*
how	كيف	*kaif*
humidity	رطوبة	*ruTooba*

hump (n, camel's back)	سنام	*sanaam*
hunger (n)	جوع	*joo'*
hurry (v, *IV*)	يسرع	*yusri'*
hurt (v, *IV*)	يؤلم	*yu'lim*
husband	زوج	*zawj, azwaaj*
hypertension	انخفاض ضغط الدم	*inkhifaaD Daght ad-dam*

I

I	أنا	*ana*
ice	ثلج	*thalj*
icon	أيقونة	*ayqoona, ayqoonaat*
idea	فكرة	*fikra, afkaar*
identical	مطابق	*muTaabiq*
if	لو	*lau*
ill (adj, sick)	مريض	*mareeD*
illegal	غير قانوني	*ghair qaanooneyy*
imagine	يتصور	*yataSaw-war*
imitation (adj, copied)	مقلد	*muqal-lad*
immediate	فوري	*fawreyy*
imperfect	معيب	*ma'eeb*
important	مهم	*muhimm*
imported (adj)	مستورد	*mustawrad*
impossible	مستحيل	*mustaHeel*

imposter	دجال	*daj-jaal, daj-jaaleen*
improve (v, *II*)	يحسن	*yuHas-sin*
in	في	*fee*
incense (aromatic)	بخور	*bukhoor*
inch	بوصة	*booSa, booSaat*
include (v, *I*)	يشمل	*yashmal*
incorrect	غير صحيح	*ghair saHeeH*
increase (v, *I* hollow)	يزيد	*yazeed*
indecent	فاضح	*faaDiH*
independent	مستقل	*musta-qill*
indigestion	عسر هضم	*'usr haDm*
inevitable	محتوم	*maHtoom*
inexpensive	رخيص	*rakheeS*
infant	طفل	*Tifl, aTfaal*
infectious	معد	*mu'di*
inflammable	سريع الاشتعال	*saree' l-ishti'aal*
inflammation (n)	ورم	*waram, awraam*
inform (v, *II*)	يبلغ	*yubal-ligh*
information	معلومات	*ma'loomaat*
ingredients	مكونات	*mukaw-winaat*
inject (v, *I*)	يحقن	*yaHqin*
injury	إصابة	*iSaaba, iSaabaat*
innocent (not guilty)	بريء	*baree'*
inoculation	تطعيم	*taT'eem*
insect	حشرة	*Hashra, Hashraat*
inside	داخل	*daakhil*

insist (v, *IV doubled*)	يصر	*yuSirr*
insomnia	أرق	*araq*
instead of	بدلا عن	*badalan 'an*
instrument	آلة	*aala, aalaat*
insult (n)	إهانة	*ihaana, ihaanaat*
insurance	تأمين	*ta'meen*
intend (v, *I defective*)	ينوي	*yanwee*
interior (adj)	داخلي	*daakhileyy*
international	دولي	*duwaleyy*
interpreter	مترجم	*mutarjim*
intestinal	معوي	*ma'aweyy*
intoxicated (adj)	سكران	*sakraan, sakaara*
intruder	دخيل	*dakheel, dukhalaa'*
invite (v, *I defective*)	يدعو	*yad'oo*
Iraq	العراق	*al-'iraaq*
Iraqi	عراقي	*'iraaqeyy, iraaqey-yeen*
Iran	إيران	*eeraan*
Iranian	إيراني	*eeraaneyy, eeraaney-yeen*
iron (n, metal)	حديد	*Hadeed*
iron (v, *I defective*; press)	يكوي	*yakwee*
Islamic	إسلامي	*islaameyy*
island	جزيرة	*jazeera, juzur*
Israel	إسرائيل	*israa-eel*
Israeli	إسرائيلي	*israa-eelee*

itching	حكة	*Hak-ka*
ivory	عاج	*'aaj*

J

jab (n, injection)	حقنة	*Huqna*
jail (n)	سجن	*sijn*
jam (n)	مربى	*murab-baa*
jasmine	ياسمين	*yasmeen*
jaw	فك	*fakk*
jellyfish	قنديل البحر	*qandeel al-baHr*
Jerusalem	القدس	*al-quds*
Jew(ish)	يهودي	*yahoodeyy, yahood*
jeweler	جوهرجي	*jawharjeyy*
job	وظيفة	*waDHeefa, waDHaa'if*
join (v, I doubled; connect)	يضم	*yaDumm*
join (v, VII doubled; enroll)	ينضم	*yanDamm*
Jordan	الأردن	*al-urdunn*
Jordanian	أردني	*urdunneyy, urdunney-yeen*
journalist	صحافي	*SaHaafeyy, SaHafey-yeen*
journey	رحلة	*riHla, riHlaat*
joy	سرور	*suroor*

jump (v, I)	يقفز	*yaqfiz*
junk	خردة	*khurda*
just (adj, fair)	عادل	*'aadil*
just (adv, only)	فقط	*faqat*
justice (n)	عدالة	*'adaala*
juvenile (adj)	صبياني	*Sibyaaneyy*

K

Kaaba (in Mecca)	الكعبة	*al-kaa'ba*
Kabyle (in Algeria)	القبائل	*al-kabaa'il*
karate	كاراتيه	*karataih*
kebob	كباب	*kabaab*
keep (v, VIII; retain)	يحتفظ	*yaIItafiDH*
keeper (n, of park, etc.)	حارس	*Haaris, Hur-raas*
kennel (n, dog)	بيت الكلب	*bayt al-kalb, buyoot al-kilaab*
kerosene	الكيروسين	*keeroseen*
ketchup	كتشب	*kitshab*
kettle	غلاية الماء	*ghallaayat al-maa'*
key	مفتاح	*muftaaH, mafaateeH*
keyboard (computer, etc.)	لوحة مفاتيح	*lawHat mafaateeH*
keyhole	ثقب المفتاح	*thuqb al-moftaaH*
khaki (n, color)	كاكي	*kaakee*

khamsin winds	رياح الخماسين	*riyaaH al-khamaaseen*
khedive	الخديوي	*al-khudaywee*
kid (child)	طفل	*Tifl, aTfaal*
kidnap (n)	اختطاف	*ikhtiTaaf*
kidney	كلية	*kilya*
kidney beans	لوبياء،	*loobyaa*
kill (v, I)	يقتل	*yaqtil*
kilogram	كيلوجرام	*keelograam*
kilometer	كيلومتر	*keelomitr*
kin (next of)	أقرب الأقرباء،	*aqrab al-aqribaa'*
kind (n, type)	نوع	*naw'*
kind (adj, good-natured)	طيب	*Tay-yib*
kindergarten	روضة أطفال	*rawDat aTfaal*
king	ملك	*malik, muluuk*
kingdom	مملكة	*mamlaka, mamaalik*
kiosk	كشك	*kushk, akshaak*
Kirman (carpets, etc.)	الكرمانية	*al-kirmaney-ya*
kiss (n)	قبلة	*qubla, qublaat*
kitchen	مطبخ	*maTbakh, maTaabikh*
kleptomania	داء السرقة	*daa' as-sirqa*
knee	ركبة	*rukba, rukab*
kneepad	وقاء الركبة	*wiqaa' ar-rukba*
kneel (v, I)	يركع	*yarka'*

knick-knacks	خردوات	*khurdawaat*
knife (n)	سكين	*sik-keen, sakaakeen*
knob (n, handle, etc.)	مقبض	*miqbaD, maqaabiD*
knob (n, of butter, etc.)	كبشة	*kabsha, kabshaat*
knock (v, I; on door, etc.)	يطرق	*yaTruq*
knot	عقدة	*'uqda*
know	يعلم	*ya'lam*
know-how	مهارة	*mahaara*
kohl	كحل	*koHl*
Koran	القرآن الكريم	*al quraan al-kareem*
kosher	مباح لليهود	*mubaaH lil-yahood*
Kurd	كردي	*kurdeyy, akraad*
Kuwait	الكويت	*al-kuwait*
Kuwaiti	كويتي	*kuwaiteyy, kuwaitey-yeen*

L

laboratory	معمل	*ma'mal, ma'aamil*
labor pains	آلام الوضع	*aalaam al-waD'*
Labor Party	حزب العمال	*Hizb al-'ummaal*
Labor Day	عيد العمال	*'eed al-'ummaal*
lace (n)	دنتلة	*dantella*
ladder	سلم	*sil-lim, salaalim*

ladle	مغرفة	*maghrafa, maghaarif*
lady	سيدة	*sayyeda, sayyedaat*
lake	بحيرة	*buHaira, buHairaat*
lamb (young sheep)	حمل	*Hamal*
lamb (meat)	ضاني صغير	*Daanee Sagheer*
lamp	مصباح	*miSbaaH, maSaabeeH*
land (n)	أرض	*arD, araaDi*
land (v, I)	يهبط	*yahbiT*
landmarks	معالم	*ma'aalim*
landscape (n, view)	منظر	*manDHar, manaaDHir*
landscape (adj. horizontal)	أفقي	*ufuqeyy*
language	لغة	*lugha, lughaat*
lantern	فانوس	*fanoos, fawaanees*
large	كبير	*kabeer*
laryngitis	التهاب الحنجرة	*iltihaab al-hanjara*
last (adj, final)	أخير	*akheer*
lasting	باق	*baaqi*
late	متأخر	*muta'akh-khir*
lather	رغوة	*raghwa*
lattice window	مشربية	*mashrabeyya, mashrabey-yaat*

laugh (v, *I*)	يضحك	*yaD-Hak*
laughter	ضحك	*DaHik*
launch (n, motorboat)	زورق سريع	*zawraq saree'*
launch (v, *IV*; new product, etc.)	يطلق	*yuTliq*
laundry (n, clothes)	غسيل	*ghaseel*
laundry (n, facility)	مغسلة	*maghsala*
lavender (n, plant)	اللاونده	*al-lawanda*
lavender (n, color)	بنفسجي فاتح	*banafsajeyy faatiH*
law	القانون	*al-qaanoon, al-qawaaneen*
lawyer	محام	*muHaami, muHaami-yeen*
laxative	ملين	*mulay-yin, mulay-yinaat*
layer (n)	طبقة	*Tabaqa, Tabaqaat*
lazy	كسول	*kasool, kasaala*
lead (n, metal)	رصاص	*ruSaaS*
leader (n, chief)	قائد	*qaa'id, qaada*
leaf	ورقة شجر	*waraqat shajar, awraaq shajar*
leak (n)	تنقيط	*tanqeeT*
lean (adj, meat)	خالي الدهن	*khaali ad-dihin*
leap (n)	قفزة	*qafza, qafzaat*
learn (v, *V*)	يتعلم	*yata'allam*

lease (v, II)	يؤجر	*yu'aj-jir*
least (adj)	أقل	*aqall*
leather	جلد	*jild*
leave (v, I; abandon)	يترك	*yatruk*
leave (n, vacation)	عطلة	*'uTla, 'uTlaat*
Lebanese	لبناني	*lubnaaneyy, lubnaaney-yeen*
Lebanon	لبنان	*lubnaan*
lecture (n)	محاضرة	*muHaadara, muHaadaraat*
left (opp. right)	يسار	*yasaar*
left-handed	أشول	*ashwal*
leg	رجل	*rijl, arjul*
legal	قانوني	*qanooneyy*
legend (myth)	أسطورة	*usToora, asaaTeer*
lemon	ليمون أصفر	*laymoon aSfar*
lemonade	ليمونادة	*laymoonada*
lend (v, I hollow)	يعير	*yu'eer*
length	طول	*Tool*
lens	عدسة	*adasa, adasaat*
Lent	صيام المسيحيين	*Siyaam al-maseeHey-yeen*
lentils	عدس	*'ads*
less (adj, fewer)	أقل	*aqall*
lesson	درس	*dars, duroos*
let (v, II; rent out)	يؤجر	*yu'aj-jir*

let (v, I; allow)	يسمح	*yasmaH*
lethal	مميت	*mumeet*
lethargy	خمول	*khumool*
letter (mail)	خطاب	*khiTaab*
letter (alphabet)	حرف	*Harf, Huroof*
lettuce	خس	*khass*
Levant	المشرق العربي	*al-mashriq al-'arabi*
level (n, height reached)	مستوى	*mustawa, mustawayaat*
library	مكتبة	*maktaba, maktabaat*
Libya	ليبيا	*leebya*
Libyan	ليبي	*leebeyy, leebey-yeen*
license	ترخيص	*tarkheeS, taraakheeS*
life	حياة	*Hayaa*
lifeboat	قارب النجاة	*qaarib an-najaah, qawaarib an-najaah*
lifebuoy	طوق النجاة	*Tawq an-najaah, aTwaaq an-najaah*
light (adj, opp. heavy)	خفيف	*khafeef*
light (n, sunlight, etc.)	ضوء	*Daw', aDwaa'*
lighthouse	فنارة	*fanaara*
lightning	برق	*barq*
like (similar to)	مثل	*mithl*

like (v, *IV doubled*; enjoy أن)	يحب أن	*yuHibb ann*
limbs	أطراف	*aTraaf*
lime (citrus fruit)	ليمون أخضر	*laymoon akhDar*
limit	حد	*Hadd, Hudood*
limp (v, *I*)	يعرج	*ya'ruj*
line	خط	*khaTT, khuTooT*
linen	بياضات	*bayaDaat*
link	وصلة	*waSla, waSlaat*
lip	شفاه	*shifaah*
lipstick	أحمر شفاة	*aHmar shifaah*
liquid	سائل	*saa'il, sawaa'il*
liquor	مشروبات روحية	*mashroobaat rawHey-ya*
list (n)	قائمة	*qaa'ima, qawaa'im*
listen (v, *VIII*)	يستمع	*yastami'*
liter	لتر	*litr*
literature	أدب	*adab*
litigation	إجراءات قضائية	*ijraa'aat qaDaa'ey-ya*
litter	زبالة	*zibaala*
little	صغير	*Sagheer*
live (v, *I*; dwell)	يسكن	*yaskun*
live (adj, wire, etc.)	حي	*Hayy*
lively	نابض	*naabiD*
liver	كبد	*kabid*

lizard	سحلية	siHliyya, saHaali
load (n, cargo, etc.)	حمل	Himl, aHmaal
loaf (n, bread)	رغيف	ragheef, arghifa
loan (n)	قرض	qarD, qurooD
local	محلي	maHal-leyy
lock (n, fastening)	قفل	qifl, aqfaal
lock (v, I)	يقفل	yaqfil
locksmith	صانع أقفال	Saani' aqfaal
lodging	مكان إقامة	makaan iqaama
logic	منطق	manTiq
lonely	وحيد	waHeed
long (adj, lengthy)	طويل	Taweel
long (v, I doubled; miss)	يحن	yaHinn
loofah	لوفة	loofa
look (v, I; see)	ينظر	yanDHur
look (n, appearance)	مظهر	maDHar, maDHaahir
look out!	احترس!	iHtaris!
loose (adj, free)	طليق	Taleeq
loose (adj, baggy)	واسع	waasi'
lorry	شاحنة	shaaHina, shaaHinaat
lose (v, I)	يفقد	yafqid
loss	خسارة	khusaara
lotus	لوتس	lootos
loud	عالي الصوت	'aali aS-Sawt

lounge (n)	قاعة جلوس	*qaa'at jiloos,* *qaa'aat jiloos*
love (n)	حب	*Hubb*
love (v, *IV doubled*)	يحب	*yuHibb*
low	منخفض	*munkhafiD*
loyal	وفي	*wafeyy*
lozenge pastille	بستيلية	*basteelya*
lubrication	تزييت	*tazyeet*
luck	حظ	*HaDH*
lucky	محظوظ	*maH-DHooDH*
luggage	أمتعة	*amti'a*
lump	ورم	*waram, awraam*
lunar	قمري	*qamareyy*
lunch	الغداء	*al-ghadaa'*
lung	رئة	*ri'a*
luxurious	فخم	*fakhm*

M

macaroni	مكرونة	*makarona*
mad (angry)	غضبان	*ghaDbaan,* *ghaDbaaneen*
mad (crazy)	مجنون	*majnoon,* *majaaneen*
magazine (periodical)	مجلة	*majal-la, majal-laat*
magistrate	قاض أول	*qaaDi aw-wal*

magnesium milk	محلول المجنيزيا	*maHlool al-magneezya*
maid	خادمة	*khadima, khadimaat*
mail (n, letters)	بريد	*bareed*
mail (v, IV)	يرسل بالبريد	*yursil bil-bareed*
main (adj, central)	رئيسي	*ra'eeseyy*
maintenance (servicing)	صيانة	*Siyaana*
maize	ذرة	*Dhur-ra*
major (at university)	التخصص الدراسي	*ut-takhaS-SuS ad-diraaseyy*
majority	أغلبية	*aghlabey-ya*
make (n, brand, etc.)	طراز	*Tiraaz, Tiraazaat*
make (v, I; manufacture, etc.)	يصنع	*yaSna'*
make-up (n, lipstick, etc.)	مكياج	*mikyaaj*
malaria	ملاريا	*malarya*
male	ذكر	*dhakar, dhukoor*
mallet	مطرقة خشبية	*miTraqa khashabey-ya*
malt	شعير	*sha'eer*
man	رجل	*rajul, rijaal*
management (n)	إدارة	*idaara*
mandatory	إجباري	*ijbaareyy*
mango	مانجو	*mango*

manicure	تجميل أظافر اليد	*tajmeel aDHaafir al-yad*
mansion	بيت فخم	*bait fakhm, buyoot fakhma*
manual (adj, by hand)	يدوي	*yadaweyy*
manual (n, booklet)	دليل مطبوع	*daleel maTboo'*
manufacture (v, *I*)	يصنع	*yaSna'*
many	كثير	*katheer*
map	خريطة	*khareeTa, kharaa'iT*
marble (n, stone)	رخام	*rukhaam*
March	مارس	*maaris*
mare	فرسة	*farasa, farasaat*
margarine	مرجرين	*marjareen*
marinate (v, *II*)	يتبل	*yutab-bil*
marine (adj)	بحري	*baHreyy*
market (n)	سوق	*sooq, aswaaq*
market (v, *II*)	يسوق	*yusaw-wiq*
marketing	تسويق	*tasweeq*
marmalade	مربى البرتقال	*murabba al-burtuqaal*
Maronite	ماروني	*maarooneyy, maarooney-yeen*
marriage	زواج	*zawaaj*
marrow	نخاع	*nukhaa'*
marry	يتزوج	*yatazaw-waj*

marvelous	مذهل	mudh-hil
mascara	مسكارا	maskaara
masculine	مذكر	mudhakkar
mash (v, I)	يهرس	yahris
mask (n)	قناع	qinaa', aqni'a
mass (church service)	قداس	qud-daas
massage	تدليك	tadleek
massive	ضخم	Dakhm
masterpiece	تحفة	tuHfa, tuHaf
mat	سجادة صغيرة	sij-jaada Sagheera
match (n, sport)	مباراة	mubaaraah
matchbox	علبة كبريت	ulbat kibreet
matches	كبريت	kibreet
material (n, fabric)	قماش	qumaash, aqmisha
mathematics	رياضيات	riyaaDiyaat
matinee	حفلة بالنهار	Hafla bin-nahaar
mattress	مرتبة	martaba, maraatib
mausoleum	ضريح	DareeH, aDreHa
maximum	أقصى	aqSaa
maybe	ربما	rub-bama
mayor	عمدة	'umda, 'umad
me	أنا	ana
meal	وجبة	wajba, wajbaat
meaning	معنى	ma'naa
measles	حصبة	HaSba
measurement	قياس	qiyaas

meat	لحم	*laHm*
Mecca	مكة	*makka*
mechanic	ميكانيكي	*mekaneeki*
medical	طبي	*Tib-beyy*
medicine	دواء	*dawaa'*
medium (adj)	متوسط	*mutawas-siT*
meet (v, *VIII defective*)	يلتقي	*yaltaqee*
melon	شمام	*sham-maam*
melt	يذوب	*yadhoob*
membership (n)	عضوية	*'uDwey-ya*
memento	تذكار	*tidhkaar*
memories	ذكريات	*dhikrayaat*
mend	يصلح	*yuSliH*
menu	قائمة	*qaa'ima*
mess (n, chaos)	فوضى	*fawDa*
message	رسالة	*risaala*
metal	معدن	*ma'dan*
middle	وسط	*waSaT*
midnight	منتصف الليل	*muntaSaf al-lail*
migraine	صداع نصفي	*Sudaa' niSfeyy*
mild	خفيف	*khafeef*
military (adj)	عسكري	*'askaree*
milk	حليب	*Haleeb*
minaret	مئذنة	*mi'dhana, ma'aadhin*
mine	لي	*lee*

mineral water	مياه معدنية	*miyaah ma'daney-ya*
minimum charge	حد أدنى	*Hadd adnaa*
mint (n, herb)	نعناع	*ni'naa'*
minute (n, time)	دقيقة	*daqeeqa, daqaa'iq*
mirage	سراب	*saraab*
mirror	مراة	*mir'aah, miraayaat*
miserable (sad)	تعيس	*ta'ees*
misfortune (bad luck)	نحس	*naHs*
missing (adj, not found)	مفقود	*mafqood, mafqoodeen*
mistake (n)	غلطة	*ghalTa, ghalaTaat*
misunderstanding	سوء فهم	*soo' fahm*
mixture	خليط	*khaleeT*
mobile	متنقل	*mutanaq-qil*
moderate (adj)	معتدل	*mu'tadil*
modern	عصري	*'aSree*
moment	لحظة	*laHdha, laHdhaat*
monastery	دير	*dair, adyira*
money	مال	*maal*
month	شهر	*shahr, shuhoor*
monthly	شهري	*shahreyy*
monuments	آثار	*aathaar*
moon	قمر	*qamar, aqmaar*
more	أكثر	*akthar*
morning	صباح	*SabaaH*

Moroccan	مغربي	*maghribeyy, maghaariba*
Morocco	المغرب	*al-maghrib*
mosque	مسجد	*masjid, masaajid*
mosquito	باعوضة	*baa'ooDa, baa'ooD*
mother (n)	أم	*umm*
mountain	جبل	*jabal, jibaal*
mouth	فم	*fam*
move (v, V)	يتحرك	*yataHar-rak*
movie	فيلم	*film, aflaam*
muezzin	مؤذن	*mu'adh-dhin, mu'adh-dhineen*
mufti	مفتي	*mufti*
mummy	مومياء	*mumya'a, mumyawaat*
muscle	عضلة	*'aDala, 'aDalaat*
museum	متحف	*matHaf, mataaHif*
music	موسيقى	*museeqa*
mystery	سر	*sirr, asraar*
myth	خرافة	*khuraafa, khurafaat*

N

name	اسم	*ism, asmaa'*
narrow	ضيق	*Day-yiq*

nationality	جنسية	jinsey-ya, jinsey-yaat
natural	طبيعي	Tabi'eyy
near	قريب	qareeb
necessary	ضروري	Darooreyy
neck	رقبة	raqba
need (n)	حاجة	Haaja, Haajaat
need (v, VIII hollow)	يحتاج	yaHtaaj
nephew (son of brother)	ابن أخ	ibn akh
nephew (son of sister)	ابن أخت	ibn ukht
nerve	عصب	'aSab, a'Saab
never	أبدا	abadan
new	جديد	jadeed
news	خبر	khabar, akhbaar
newspaper	جريدة	jareeda, jaraa'id
newsstand	كشك الجرائد	kushk al-jaraa'id
next	تال	taali
niece (daughter of brother)	بنت أخ	bint akh
niece (daughter of sister)	بنت أخت	bint ukht
night	ليل	lail, layaali
Nile	النيل	an-neel
nobody	لا أحد	laa aHad
noise	ضجيج	Dajeej
nomad	رحال	raH'Haal

normal	عادي	'aadeyy
north	شمال	shamaal
nose	أنف	anf
nothing	لا شئ	laa shai'
now	الآن	al-aan
Nubia	النوبة	an-nooba
Nubian	نوبي	noobeyy, noobey-yeen
nuisance (adj)	مزعج	muz'ij
number	رقم	raqm, arqaam
nurse	ممرضة	mumar-riDa, momar-riDaat
nuts (adj, crazy)	مخبول	makhbool
nuts (n, walnuts, etc.)	مكسرات	mukas-saraat

O

oasis	واحة	waaHa, waaHaat
obelisk	مسلة	misal-la, misal-laat
obligatory	اجباري	ijbaareyy
obtain	يحصل على	yaHSul 'alaa
obvious	واضح	waaDiH
occasion	مناسبة	munaasaba, munaasabaat
ocean	محيط	muHeeT, muHeeTaat

offence (n, crime)	جريمة	*jareema, jaraa'im*
offence (n, insult)	إساءة	*isaa'a, isaa'aat*
offer (n)	عرض	*'arD, 'urooD*
offer (v, I)	يعرض	*ya'raD*
office	مكتب	*maktab, makaatib*
officer (military)	ضابط	*DaabiT, Dub-baaT*
oil	زيت	*zait, zuyoot*
okra	بامية	*bamya*
old (object)	قديم	*qadeem*
old (person)	مسن	*ɪnusinn*
olive	زيتونة	*zaitoona, zaitoon*
Oman	عمان	*'umaan*
Omani	عماني	*'umaaneyy, umaaney-yeen*
on	على	*'ala*
once	مرة	*mar-ra*
onion	بصل	*baSal*
only	فقط	*faqaT*
open (adj)	مفتوح	*maftooH*
operation	عملية	*'amaley-ya, 'amaley-yaat*
opportunity	فرصة	*furSa, furaS*
opposite	عكس	*'aks*
optician	نظاراتي	*naDH-DHaraati*
optional	اختياري	*ikhti-yaareyy*
or	أو	*aw*

orange (adj, color)	برتقالي	*burtuqaaleyy*
orange (n, fruit)	برتقال	*burtuqaala, burtuqaal*
order (n, method)	نظام	*niDHaam*
order (v, I; demand)	يأمر	*ya'mur*
ordinary	عادي	*'aadeyy*
organic	عضوي	*'uDwee*
organize (v, II)	ينظم	*yunaDH-DHim*
oriental	شرقي	*sharqeyy*
orientalist	مستشرق	*mustashriq, mustashriqeen*
original (adv)	أصلي	*aSleyy*
ornamental	زخرفي	*zukhrufi*
other	آخر	*aakhar*
ours	لنا	*lina*
outside	في الخارج	*fil-khaarij*
oven	فرن	*furn*
overland	برا	*bar-ran*
oversight	سهو	*sahw*
owe	يدين	*yadeen*
owner	مالك	*maalik*

P

pack (v)	يحزم	*yaHzim*
package (n)	طرد	*Tard, Turood*

package (v, *II*)	يغلف	*yughal-lif*
padlock (n)	قفل	*qifl, aqfaal*
page (of book, etc.)	صفحة	*SafHa, SafaHaat*
pain (n)	ألم	*alam*
palace	قصر	*qaSr, quSoor*
pale (adj)	شاحب	*shaaHib*
Palestine	فلسطين	*falasTeen*
Palestinian	فلسطيني	*falasTeeneyy, falasTeeney-yeen*
palm (n, anatomical)	كف	*kaff*
palm tree	نخلة	*nakhla, nakhl*
pamphlet	كتيب	*kutay-yib*
panic (n)	هلع	*hala'*
paper (n, sheet, etc.)	ورق	*waraq, awraaq*
papyrus	ورق البردي	*waraq al-bardi*
paradise	فردوس	*firdaws*
parasite	طفيلي	*Tofaileyy*
pardon (n, amnesty)	عفو	*'afw*
parents	أبوين	*abawain*
park (n, gardens)	حديقة	*Hadeeqa, Hadaa'iq*
park (v, *I doubled*; cars, etc.)	يصف	*yaSuff*
part (n, section)	جزء	*juz', ajzaa'*
partner (n)	شريك	*shareek, shurakaa'*
party (n, ball)	حفلة	*Hafla, Haflaat*
party (n, political)	حزب	*Hizb, aHzaab*

pass (n, permit)	تصريح	taSreeH, taSaareeH
pass (v, I doubled; go past)	يمر	yamurr
passenger	راكب	raakib, ruk-kaab
passport	جواز سفر	jawaaz safar
past (adj)	ماض	maaDi
paternal	أبوي	abaweyy
path	ممر	mamarr
patience (n)	صبر	Sabr
patient (n, sick person)	مريض	mareeD, marDaa
pay (v, I)	يدفع	yadfa'
peace	سلام	salaam
pearl	لؤلؤة	lu'lu'a, lu'lu'
peas	بازلاء	bazilaa'
pencil	قلم رصاص	qalam ruSaaS
people	ناس	naas
pepper (n)	فلفل	filfil
perfect	كامل	kaamil
performance	عرض	'arD, urooD
permit (v, I)	يسمح	yasmaH
person	شخص	shakhS, ash-khaaS
Pharaonic	فرعوني	fir'awneyy
pharmacy	صيدلية	Saydaley-ya, Saydaley-yaat
phonecard	كارت التليفون	kart at-tilifon

photographer	مصور	muSaw-wir, muSaw-wireen
pick (v, *VIII hollow*; choose)	يختار	yakhtaar
picture (n, photo, etc.)	صورة	Soora, Suwar
piece (n)	قطعة	qiT'a, qiTa'
pierce	يثقب	yathqub
pilgrim	حاج	Haajj, Hujjaaj
pilgrimage (to Mecca)	الحج	al-Hajj
pill	قرص	qurS, aqraaS
pin (n)	دبوس	dab-boos, dabaabees
place (n, location)	مكان	makaan, amaakin
plant (n)	نبات	nabaat, nabaataat
plant (v, *I*)	يزرع	yazra'
plate (n, dish)	صحن	saHn, SuHoon
platform (n, for train)	رصيف	raSeef, arSifa
play (n)	مسرحية	masraHey-ya, masraHey-yaat
play (v, *I*)	يلعب	yal'ab
plenty	كثير	katheer
plug (n)	سدادة	sad-daada
plumber	سباك	sab-baak
pocket (n)	جيب	jaib, juyoob
point (n, dot)	نقطة	nuqTa, nuqaTT
point (v, *IV hollow*)	يشير	yusheer
polite	مؤدب	mu'ad-dab

pomegranate	رمان	*rum-maan*
pool (n, pond, etc.)	بركة	*birka, birak*
popular	شعبي	*sha'bee*
port	ميناء	*meena', mawaani'*
porter	حمال	*Ham-maal, Ham-maaleen*
positive	ايجابي	*eejaabee*
possibility	احتمال	*iHtimaal*
post office	مكتب البريد	*maktab al-bareed*
postcard	بطاقة بريدية	*biTaqa bareedey-ya*
pottery	فخار	*fukh-khaar*
powder	مسحوق	*masHooq, masaaHeeq*
prawns (shrimp)	جمبري	*jambaree* (coll.)
pray (v, II defective)	يصلي	*yuSal-lee*
precious	نفيس	*nafees*
precisely	بدقة	*bi-diq-qa*
prefer	يفضل	*yufaD-Dil*
pregnant	حامل	*Haamil*
prescription	روشتة	*rooshet-ta*
press (n, media)	صحافة	*SaHaafa*
press (n, printing)	مطبعة	*maTba'a, maTaabi'*
press (v, I defective; iron)	يكوي	*yakwee*
press (v, I; push)	يدفع	*yadfa'*
pretty	جميل	*jameel*
prey	فريسة	*fareesa*

price (n)	سعر	si'r, as'aar
prince	أمير	ameer, umaraa'
princess	أميرة	ameera, ameeraat
prison	سجن	sijn, sujoon
private	خاص	khaaS
problem	مشكلة	mushkila, mashaakil
professional	محترف	muHtarif, muHtarifeen
prohibited	ممنوع	mamnoo'
promise (n)	وعد	wa'd, wu'ood
proof	برهان	burhaan
prophet	رسول	rasool
province	إقليم	iqleem, aqaaleem
provincial	ريفي	reefeyy
pull (v, I)	يسحب	yasHab
puncture (n)	ثقب	thuqb, thuqoob
pure	نقي	naqeyy
purple	بنفسجي	banafsajeyy
push (v, I)	يدفع	yadfa'
put	يضع	yadaa'
pyramid	هرم	haram, ahraam

Q

Qatar	قطر	qaTar

Qatari	قطري	*qaTareyy, qaTarey-yeen*
quaint	طريف	*Tareef*
quality (n)	جودة	*jawda*
quantity (n)	كمية	*kim-mey-ya*
quarrel (v, *VI*)	يتشاجر	*yatashaajar*
quarter (n)	ربع	*rub'*
queen	ملكة	*malika, malikaat*
question (n)	سؤال	*su'aal, as'ila*
quick	سريع	*saree'*
quiet (adj)	هادئ	*haadi'*
quit (v, *I*)	يهجر	*yahjur*

R

rabbi	حاخام	*Haakhaam*
rabbit	أرنب	*arnab, araanib*
race (n, running, etc.)	سباق	*sibaaq, sibaaqaat*
railroad	سكة حديد	*sikka Hadeed*
rain (n)	مطر	*maTar*
raise (v, *I*)	يرفع	*yarfa'*
raisin	زبيب	*zibeeb*
Ramadan	رمضان	*ramaDaan*
rare (uncommon)	نادر	*naadir*
rash (n)	طفح جلدي	*TafH jildee*
rat	جرذ	*jurdh, jurdhaan*

rate (n)	معدل	mu'ad-dal
raw	نيء	nayy'
razor	موس حلاقة	moos Hilaaqa
reach (v, I assimilated)	يصل	yaSil
read (v, I)	يقرأ	yaqra'
ready (adj)	جاهز	jaahiz
real	حقيقي	Haqeeqeyy
reason (n, cause)	سبب	sabab, asbaab
reasonable	معقول	ma'qool
rebate	خصم	khaSm
receipt	إيصال	eeSaal, eeSaalaat
receive	يستلم	yastalim
reception (n, hotel)	استقبال	istiqbaal
recipe	وصفة	waSfa, waSfaat
recommendation	توصية	tawSey-ya
recover (from illness)	يشفى	yushfa
rectangle	مستطيل	mustaTeel, mustaTeelaat
reduce (v, II)	يقلل	yuqal-lil
reef	صخور بحرية	Sukhoor baHrey-ya
refill (v, I)	يملأ	yamla'
refresh (v, IV)	ينعش	yun'ish
refreshments	مرطبات	muraT-Tibaat
refuse (v, I)	يرفض	yarfuD
regional	إقليمي	iqleemee
regret (v, I)	يأسف	ya'saf

relationship	علاقة	*'ilaaqa, 'ilaaqaat*
relative (n)	قريب	*qareeb, aqaarib*
relax(v, *VIII*)	يستجم	*yastajim*
reliable	موثوق به	*mawthooq bih*
relic	أثر	*athar, aathaar*
religion	دين	*deen, adyaan*
remain (v, *I defective*)	يبقى	*yabqa*
remedy (n)	علاج	*'ilaaj*
remember	يتذكر	*yatadhak-kar*
remove	يبعد	*yub'id*
rent (v, *II*)	يؤجر	*yu'aj-jir*
repair (n)	تصليح	*taSleeH*
repeat (v, *II*)	يكرر	*yukar-rir*
repellent (n)	طارد	*Taarid*
reply (n)	رد	*radd, rudood*
reply (v, *I doubled*)	يرد	*yarudd*
reporter	صحفي	*SaHafee, SaHafeeyeen*
representative (n)	مندوب	*mandoob, mandoobeen*
request (n)	طلب	*Talab, Talabaat*
request (v, *I*)	يطلب	*yaTlub*
rescue (n)	إنقاذ	*inqaadh*
reservation (n)	حجز	*Hajz, Hujuzaat*
residential	سكني	*sakaneyy*
resignation	استقالة	*istiqaala*

resolve (v, *I doubled*)	يحل	*yaHill*
resort (n)	منتجع	*muntaja',* *muntaja'aat*
respect (n)	احترام	*iHtiraam*
respiratory	تنفسي	*tanaf-fuseyy*
responsible	مسؤول	*mas'ool*
rest (v, *X hollow*)	يستريح	*yastareeH*
restaurant	مطعم	*maT'am,* *maTaa'im*
restoration	تجديد	*tajdeed*
result (n)	نتيجة	*nateeja, nataa'ij*
retirement (from work)	تقاعد	*taqaa'ud*
return (n)	عودة	*'awda*
return (v, *I hollow*)	يعود	*ya'ood*
reverse (n)	عكس	*'aks*
reward (n)	مكافأة	*mukaafa'a,* *mukaafa'aat*
rice	رز	*ruzz*
riding (n)	ركوب الخيل	*rukoob al-khail*
right (opp. left)	يمين	*yameen*
right (correct)	صحيح	*saHeeH*
right (n, entitlement)	حق	*Haqq, Huqooq*
rise (v, *VIII*)	يرتفع	*yartafi'*
risk (n)	مجازفة	*mujaazafa,* *mujaazafaat*
road	طريق	*Tareeq, Turuq*

rock	صخرة	*Sakhra, Sokhoor*
roof	سقف	*saqf, suqoof*
room (n, hotel, etc.)	حجرة	*Hujra, Hujraat*
root (n)	جذر	*jidhr, judhoor*
rope	حبل	*Habl, Hibaal*
rosary	سبحة	*sibHa*
rose	زهرة	*zahra, zuhoor*
Rosetta	رشيد	*rasheed*
rough (adj, not smooth)	خشن	*khashin*
round (adj, spherical)	مستدير	*mustadeer*
round-trip	ذهاب وعودة	*dhihaab wa 'awda*
route (n)	خط سير	*khaTT sair*
rubber ring	عوامة	*'aw-waama*
ruby (n)	ياقوت	*yaaqoot*
rug	سجادة	*sij-jaada, sajaajeed*
ruins	أطلال	*aTlaal*
run (v, *I defective*)	يجري	*yajree*
run (v, *IV hollow; operate*)	يدير	*yudeer*
rural	قروي	*qaraweyy*
rush (v, *IV*)	يسرع	*yusri'*
rustic	ريفي	*reefeyy*
rye (n)	شيلم	*shailam*

S

sacred (adj)	مقدس	*muqad-das*

sad	حزين	*Hazeen*
saddle (n)	سرج	*sarj*
safe (adj, opp. risky)	مأمون	*ma'moon*
safe (n, secure box)	خزنة	*khazna, khizan*
saffron	زعفران	*za'faraan*
sail (n)	شراع	*shiraa'*
sailor	بحار	*baH-Haar, baH-Haara*
saint	قديس	*qid-dees, qid-deeseen*
sale (n, discount)	أوكازيون	*okazyon, okazyonaat*
salesman	مندوب مبيعات	*mandoob mabee'aat, mandoobeen*
salt (n)	ملح	*malH, amlaaH*
same (adj)	ذاته	*dhaatuh*
sample (n)	عينة	*'ay-yina, 'ay-yinaat*
sample (v)	يجرب	*yujar-rib*
sand (n)	رمل	*raml, rimaal*
sanitary	صحي	*SiH-Heyy*
sarcophagus	تابوت حجري	*taaboot Hajareyy*
satellite	قمر صناعي	*qamar Sinaa'eyy*
satisfaction	رضا	*riDaa*
saucepan	كسرولة	*kasarol-la*
Saudi (Arabia)	السعودية	*as-sa'oodey-ya*
Saudi (Arabian)	سعودي	*sa'oodeyy, sa'oodey-yeen*

sausage	سجق	*sujuq*
save (v, IV; rescue)	ينقذ	*yunqidh*
save (v, VIII; set aside)	يدخر	*yad-dakhir*
say (v, I hollow)	يقول	*yaqool*
scalp (n)	فروة الرأس	*farwat ar-ra's*
scenery	منظر	*manDHar, manaaDHir*
school (n)	مدرسة	*madrasa, madaaris*
screen (n)	ستار	*sitaar*
scuba diving (n)	غطس	*ghaTs*
sea	بحر	*baHr*
search (v, I)	يبحث	*yabHath*
season (n, spring, etc.)	فصل	*faSl, fuSool*
season (v, II; add spices)	يتبل	*yutab-bil*
seat (n)	كرسي	*kurseyy, karaasee*
second (n, after first)	ثان	*thaani*
second (n, time)	ثانية	*thaanya, thawaani*
secret (n)	سر	*sirr, asraar*
secret (adj)	سري	*sir-reyy*
security (n)	أمن	*amn*
sedative	مسكن	*musak-kin, musak-kinaat*
see (v, I defective)	يرى	*yara*
seizure (n, fit)	نوبة	*nawba, nawbaat*
select (v, VIII; hollow)	يختار	*yakhtaar*
sell (v, I; hollow)	يبيع	*yabee'*

send (v, *IV*)	يرسل	*yursil*
sensitive	حساس	*Has-saas*
separately	منفصلين	*munfaSileen*
serious	جدي	*jid-deyy*
service (n, favor)	خدمة	*khidma, khidmaat*
set (adj, fixed)	محدد	*muHad-dadd*
set (n, specific group)	طقم	*Taqm, aTqum*
set (v, *I*; clock, etc.)	يضبط	*yaDbuT*
set (v, *VIII*; place aside)	يحتجز	*yaHtajiz*
settle (v, *II*; pay)	يسدد	*yusad-did*
shade (n)	ظل	*DHil, DHilaal*
shape (n)	شكل	*shakl, ashkaal*
shares (n)	أسهم	*ashum*
shark	سمكة القرش	*samakat al-qirsh*
shave (v, *I*)	يحلق	*yaHlaq*
sheet	ملاءة	*milaa'a, milaa'aat*
sheik	شيخ	*shaikh, shuyookh*
ship (n)	سفينة	*safeena, sufun*
shipment (n)	شحنة	*shuHna, shuHnaat*
shirt (n)	قميص	*qameeS, qumSaan*
shock (n)	صدمة	*Sadma, Sadmaat*
shoe	حذاء	*Hidhaa', aHdheya*
shoelace	رباط الحذاء	*ribaaT al-hizhaa'*
shop (n)	محل	*maHal, maHal-laat*
shop (v, *V*)	يتسوق	*yatasaw-waq*

shopping mall	سوق مول	*sooq mol*
short (adj, opp. long)	قصير	*qaSeer*
shoulder (n)	كتف	*katif, aktaaf*
show (n, spectacle)	عرض	*'arD, 'urooD*
show (v, I; display)	يعرض	*ya'riD*
shower (n)	دش	*dush*
shrimp	جمبري	*gambari (coll.)*
shrine	ضريح	*DareeH, aDreHa*
shut (v, I)	يقفل	*yaqfil*
sick	مريض	*mareeD*
side (n)	ناحية	*naaHiya, nawaaHi*
sign (n, display board)	لافتة	*laafita, laafitaat*
sign (n, mark)	علامة	*'alaama, 'alaamaat*
sign (v, II; check, etc.)	يوقع	*yuwaq-qi'*
signature	توقيع	*tawqee', tawqee'aat*
silence (n)	صمت	*Samt*
silk (adj)	حريري	*Hareereyy*
silk (n)	حرير	*Hareer*
silver (adj)	فضي	*faD-Deyy*
silver (n)	فضة	*faD-Da*
similarity	تشابه	*tashaabuh*
simple	بسيط	*baseeT*
sing (v, II defective)	يغني	*yughan-nee*
sink (n)	حوض	*HawD, aHwaaD*
sister	أخت	*ukht, akhawaat*

sit (v, *I*)	يجلس	*yajlis*
size (n)	حجم	*Hajm, aHjaam*
skill (n)	مهارة	*mahaara, mahaaraat*
skim (adj, milk)	مقشود	*maqshood*
skin (n)	جلد	*jild*
skirt	جونلة / جيبة	*gunel-la, gunel-laat/ jeeba, jeebaat*
sky	سماء	*samaa', samawaat*
sleep (v, *I hollow*)	ينام	*yanaam*
sleeve (n)	كم	*kumm, akmaam*
slice (n)	شريحة	*shareeHa, sharaa'iH*
slip (v, *VII*; lose footing)	ينزلق	*yanzaliq*
slippers	شبشب	*shibshib, shabaashib*
slow (adj)	بطيء	*baTee'*
small (adj)	صغير	*Sagheer*
smell (n, scent)	رائحة	*raa'iHa, rawaa'iH*
smell (n, sense)	شم	*shamm*
smell (v, *I doubled*)	يشم	*yashimm*
smile (n)	ابتسامة	*ibtisaama, ibtisaamaat*
smoke (n)	دخان	*dokh-khaan*
smoke (v, *II*)	يدخن	*yudakh-khin*
smooth (adj)	ناعم	*naa'im*

snorkel (n)	أنبوب التنفس	*unboob at-tanaf-fus*
soap (n)	صابون	*Saaboon*
soccer	كرة القدم	*kurat al-qadam*
soft	طري	*Tareyy*
soldier (n)	جندي	*jundeyy, junood*
solution (n, answer)	حل	*Hall, Huloot*
solution (n, liquid)	محلول	*maHlool*
some	بعض	*baa'D*
son	ابن	*ibn, abnaa'*
song	أغنية	*ughneya, aghaani*
sore	ملتهب	*multahib*
sorry	آسف	*aasif*
sound (n)	صوت	*Sawt, aSwaat*
soup	شوربة	*shorba*
speak (v, *V*)	يتكلم	*yatakal-lam*
speed (n)	سرعة	*sur'a*
spices (n)	توابل	*tawaabil*
spoon (n)	ملعقة	*mil'aqa, malaa'iq*
sport (n)	رياضة	*riyaaDa*
spot (n, stain)	بقعة	*buq'a, buqa'*
spot (v, *I*; see)	يلمح	*yalmaH*
spring (n, season)	الربيع	*ar-rabee'*
square (n)	مربع	*muraba', murab-ba'aat*
stamp (n, postage)	طابع بريد	*Taabi' bareed*
stand (n, position)	موقف	*mawqif, mawaaqif*

stand (v, I assimilated)	يقف	*yaqif*
star (n)	نجم	*nijm, nujoom*
start (v, I)	يبدأ	*yabda'*
station (n)	محطة	*maHaT-Ta, maHaT-Taat*
station (n, police)	قسم البوليس	*qism al-bolees*
statue	تمثال	*timthaal, tamaatheel*
stay (v, I defective)	يبقى	*yabqa*
step (n)	خطوة	*khaTwa, khaTwaat*
stewardess	مضيفة	*maDeefa, maDeefaat*
stomach (n)	معدة	*mu'ida*
stone (n)	حجر	*Hajar, aHjaar*
stop (v, I assimilated)	يقف	*yaqif*
store (n)	محل	*maHall, maHal-laat*
storm (n)	عاصفة	*'aaSifa, 'awaaSif*
story (n, level)	طابق	*Taabiq, Tawaabiq*
story (n, tale)	قصة	*qiS-Sa, qiSaS*
straight (direct)	مباشر	*mubaashir*
strange (adj)	غريب	*ghareeb*
strawberry	فراولة	*farawla*
strength	قوة	*quw-wa, quw-waat*
stretcher	نقالة	*naq-qaala*

string (cord)	خيط	*khaiT, khuyooT*
strong	قوي	*qaweyy*
student (n)	طالب	*Taalib, Talaba*
study (v, I)	يدرس	*yadrus*
style (n)	طراز	*Tiraaz, Tiraazat*
subject (n, topic)	موضوع	*mawDoo', mawDoo'aat*
succeed (v, I; opp. fail)	ينجح	*yanjaH*
such	كهذا	*ka-haazha*
Sudan	السودان	*as-soodaan*
Sudanese	سوداني	*soodaaneyy, soodaaney-yeen*
sugar (n)	سكر	*suk-kar*
suggestion	اقتراح	*iqtiraaH, iqtiraaHaat*
suit (n, clothing)	بذلة	*badhla*
suitable	مناسب	*munaasib*
suite (hotel)	جناح	*jinaaH, ajniHa*
sultan	سلطان	*sulTaan*
sum (n, total)	مجموع	*majmoo'*
summer	صيف	*Saif*
sun (n)	شمس	*shams*
sunburn (n)	حروق الشمس	*Hurooq ash-shams*
sunrise	شروق	*shorooq*
sunset	غروب	*ghoroob*
sure	واثق	*waathiq*

surgery (n, clinic)	عيادة	'iyaada, 'iyaadaat
surgery (n, operation)	جراحة	jiraaHa, jiraaHaat
surprise (n)	مفاجأة	mufaaja'a, mufaaja'aat
swallow (v, I; ingest)	يبلع	yabla'
sweet (adj)	حلو	Hulw
swim (v, I)	يسبح	yasbaH
Syria	سوريا	surey-yaa
Syrian	سوري	sureyy, surey-yeen
syringe (n)	حقنة	Huqna, Huqan
system	نظام	niDHaam, anDHima

T

table (n)	مائدة	maa'ida, mawaa'id
tablet	قرص	qurS, aqraaS
tailor (n)	ترزي	tarzi, tarzey-ya
take (v, I)	يأخذ	ya'khudh
talk (v, V)	يتكلم	yatakal-lam
tapestry	نسيج مزخرف	naseej muzakhraf
taste (n, sense)	تذوق	tadhaw-wuq
tax (n)	ضريبة	Dareeba, Daraa'ib
tea (n)	شاي	shaay
teach (v, II)	يعلم	yu'al-lim

teacher	معلم	mu'al-lim, mu'al-limeen
tear (n, drop)	دمعة	dam'a, dumoo'
tear (v, II; shred)	يمزق	yumaz-ziq
teenager	مراهق	muraahiq, muraahiqeen
tell (v, IV)	يخبر	yukhbir
temperature	درجة الحرارة	darajat al-Haraara
temple	معبد	ma'bad, ma'aabid
temporary	مؤقت	mu'aq-qat
tenant (n)	مستأجر	musta'jir, musta'jireen
tent	خيمة	khaima, khiyaam
terminal (n, airport)	مبنى المطار	mabna al-maTaar
terminal (n, bus)	موقف الأوتوبيس	mawqaf al-otobees
terrace (balcony)	شرفة	shurfa, shurfaat
terrible	فظيع	faDHee'
terrific	رائع	raa'i
test (n)	اختبار	ikhtibaar, ikhtibaaraat
textile	نسيج	naseej
thankful (adj)	شاكر	shaakir
theater (n, plays, etc.)	مسرح	masraH, masaariH
theater (n, surgeries, etc.)	غرفة العمليات	ghurfat al-'amaley-yaat
therapy	علاج	'ilaaj

there	هناك	*Hunaak*
thick	سميك	*sameek*
thief (n)	لص	*liSS, luSooS*
thin	نحيف	*naHeef*
thing	شيء	*shai', ashyaa'*
thirsty	عطشان	*'atshaan*
this	هذا	*haadha*
thoroughbred	أصيل	*aSeel*
throat	زور	*zawr*
through (prep)	خلال	*khilaal*
throw (v, I defective)	يرمي	*yarmee*
thyme	زعتر	*za'tar*
ticket (n)	تذكرة	*tadhkara, tadhaakir*
tie (n, neck)	كرافتة	*karavatta*
tie (v, I)	يربط	*yarbuT*
tight	ضيق	*Day-yiq*
tights	كولونات	*kolonaat*
time (n, eras, etc.)	زمن	*zaman*
time (n, of day)	وقت	*waqt*
tip (n, gratuity)	إكرامية	*ikramey-ya, ikramey-yaat*
tire (n)	إطار	*iTaar, iTaaraat*
tire (v, I)	يتعب	*yat'ab*
tired (adj)	تعبان	*ta'baan*
today	اليوم	*al-yawm*

together (adj)	معا	ma'an
tomato	طماطم	TamaaTim
tomb	مقبرة	maqbara, maqaabir
tomorrow	غدا	ghadan
tongue	لسان	lisaan, alsina
tonight	الليلة	al-laila
tooth	سنة	sin-na, asnaan
top (n)	أعلى	a'la
total (adj, entire)	تام	taam
total (n)	مجموع	majmoo'
touch (v, I)	يلمس	yalmis
tour (n)	جولة	jawla, jawlaaat
tour (v, V; visit)	يتجول	yatajaw-wal
tourist (n)	سائح	saa'iH, suyauH
tow (v, I doubled)	يجر	yajurr
towards (prep)	نحو	naHwa
towel	منشفة	minshafa, manaashif
tower	برج	burj, abraaj
town	مدينة	madeena, mudun
trader	تاجر	taajir, tuj-jaar
traditional (adj)	تقليدي	taqleedeyy
traffic (n, cars, etc.)	مرور	muroor
train (n)	قطار	qiTaar, qiTaaraa
train (v, V)	يتدرب	yatadar-rab

transfer (n)	تحويل	*taHweel, taHweelaat*
translator	مترجم	*mutarjim, mutarjimeen*
transportation	وسيلة تنقل	*waseelat tanaq-qul*
trash (n)	زبالة	*zibaala*
travel (v, III)	يسافر	*yusaafir*
traveler's checks	شيكات سياحية	*sheekaat seyaaHey-ya*
treat (v, III; behave towards)	يعامل	*yu'aamil*
treat (n, reward)	مكافأة	*mukaafa'a*
tree	شجرة	*shajara, ashjaar*
triangle	مثلث	*muthal-lath, muthal-lathaat*
tribe	قبيلة	*qabeela, qabaa'il*
trim (n, hair, etc.)	تشذيب	*tash-dheeb*
trip (n, voyage)	رحلة	*riHla, riHlaat*
trip (v, stumble)	يتعثر	*yata'ath-thar*
trouble (n)	متاعب	*mataa'ib*
truck (n)	شاحنة	*shaaHina, shaaHinaaat*
true	حقيقي	*Haqeeqeyy*
trust (v)	يثق	*yathiq*
try (v)	يحاول	*yuHaawil*
Tunis	تونس	*toonis*
Tunisian	تونسي	*tooniseyy, toonisey-yeen*

tunnel (n)	نفق	*nafaq, anfaaq*
Turkey	تركيا	*torkeya*
turkey	ديك رومي	*deek roomeyy*
turn (v, *I doubled*; go around)	يلف	*yaliff*
turn (v, *II*; transform)	يحول	*yuHaw-wil*
twin	توأم	*taw'am, tawaa'im*
type (n)	نوع	*naw', anwaa'*

U

ulcer	قرحة	*qurHa*
ultimate (adj)	أخير	*akheer*
umbrella	مظلة	*miDHal-la, miDHal-laat*
unable	غير قادر	*ghair qaadir*
unattended	بلا رقابة	*bilaa riqaaba*
unbearable	لا يطاق	*laa yuTaaq*
unbelievable	لا يصدق	*laa yuSad-daq*
uncertain	غير واثق	*ghair waathiq*
uncle (maternal)	خال	*khaal, khilaan*
uncle (paternal)	عم	*'amm, 'amaam*
uncomfortable	غير مريح	*ghair mureeH*
uncommon	غير مألوف	*ghair ma'loof*
unconscious	في إغماءة	*fee ighmaa'a*
uncover (v, *I*)	يكشف	*yakshif*
undecided	متردد	*mutarad-did*

under (prep)	تحت	*taHt*
undergraduate	طالب في الجامعة	*Taalib fee l-jaami'a*
understand (v, I)	يفهم	*yafham*
uneasy	قلق	*qaliq*
unemployment (n)	بطالة	*biTaala*
unexpected (adj)	مفاجئ	*mufaaji'*
unhappy	حزين	*Hazeen*
unhealthy	غير صحي	*ghair SiH-Hi*
United Arab Emirates	الإمارات العربية المتحدة	*al-imaaraat al-'arabey-ya al-muttaHida*
United Nations	الأمم المتحدة	*al-umam al-muttaHida*
United States	الولايات المتحدة	*al-wilaayaat al-muttaHida*
university	جامعة	*jaami'a, jaami'aat*
unknown (adj)	مجهول	*majhool*
unlucky (adj)	سيء الحظ	*say-yi' al-HaDH*
unofficial	غير رسمي	*ghair rasmeyy*
unreal	وهمي	*wahmeyy*
unreasonable	غير معقول	*ghair ma'qool*
unstable	متقلب	*mutaqal-lib*
unsuitable	غير مناسب	*ghair munaasib*
until (prep)	إلى أن	*ila 'an*
untrue	كاذب	*kaadhib*
unusual (adj)	نادر	*naadir*

up	فوق	*fawq*
upgrade (n)	ترقية	*tarqeya*
uprising	انتفاضة	*intifaaDa*
urban (adj)	مدني	*madaneyy*
use (n, benefit)	فائدة	*faa'ida, fawaa'id*
use (v, *X*)	يستخدم	*yastakhdim*
useful	مفيد	*mufeed*

V

vacancy (in hotel)	غرف خالية	*ghuraf khaaliya*
vacancy (for job)	وظائف خالية	*waDHaa'if khaaliya*
vacate (v, *IV defective*)	يخلي	*yukhlee*
vacation (n)	عطلة	*'uTla, 'uTlaat*
vaccination	تطعيم	*taT'eem*
vague (adj)	غامض	*ghaamiD*
vain	مغرور	*maghroor*
valid	صالح	*SaaliH*
valley	واد	*waadi, widyaan*
valuable	ثمين	*thameen*
vanish	يختفي	*yakhtafee*
veal	بتللو	*bitel-lo*
vegetable(s)	خضار	*khuDaar*
vegetarian	نباتي	*nabaateyy*

vehicle	سيارة	*say-yaara, say-yaaraat*
veil (n)	حجاب	*Hijaab*
vein (anatomy)	وريد	*wareed, awrida*
velvet	قطيفة	*qaTeefa*
ventilation	تهوية	*tahwiya*
verbal	شفوي	*shafaweyy*
vernacular (language)	العامية	*al-'aamey-ya*
veterinary	بيطري	*baiTareyy*
view (n, opinion)	رأي	*ra'yy, aaraa'*
view (n, scenery)	منظر	*manDHar, manaaDHir*
vigilance	يقظة	*yaqDHa*
village	قرية	*qarya, quraa*
vinegar	خل	*khall*
visa	تأشيرة	*ta'sheera, ta'sheeraat*
visit (n)	زيارة	*ziyaara, ziyaaraat*
voice (n)	صوت	*Sawt, aSwaat*
void (adj, invalidated)	باطل	*baaTil*
voluntary (n)	تطوعي	*tataw-wu'eyy*
volunteer (n)	متطوع	*mutaTaw-wi', mutaTaw-wi'een*
vomit (v, V)	يتقيأ	*yataqay-ya'*
vulgar	سوقي	*sooqeyy*

W

wage (n, salary)	أجر	*ajr, ujoor*
Wailing Wall	حائط المبكى	*Haa'iT al-mabka*
waist	خصر	*khaSr*
wait (v, VIII)	ينتظر	*yantaDHir*
waiter (n)	جرسون	*garsoon*
wake (v, X)	يستيقظ	*yastaiqiDH*
walk (v, I defective)	يمشي	*yamshee*
wall	حائط	*Haa'iT, Hawaa'iT*
wallet	حافظة	*HaafiDHa*
want (v, IV hollow)	يريد	*yureed*
war	حرب	*Harb*
ward (hospital)	عنبر	*'anbar, 'anaabir*
warm (adj)	دافئ	*daafi'*
warranty	ضمان	*Damaan*
wash (v, I)	يغسل	*yaghsil*
washing machine	غسالة ملابس	*ghas-saalat malaabis*
watch (n, on wrist)	ساعة يد	*saa'at yad*
watch (v, III; observe)	يراقب	*yuraaqib*
water (n)	ماء	*maa'*
waterfall	شلال	*shal-laal, shal-laalaat*
wave (n, in sea)	موجة	*mawja, amwaaj*
wave (v, II; with hand)	يلوح	*yulaw-wiH*

wax (n)	شمع	sham'
way (n, method)	طريقة	Tareeqa, Turuq
way (n, route)	طريق	Tareeq, Turuq
weak	ضعيف	Da'eef
wealthy	غني	ghaneyy
wear	يلبس	yalbus
weather (n)	جو	jaww
web	شبكة	shabaka
wedding (n)	زفاف	zifaaf
week	أسبوع	usboo', asaabee'
weekly	أسبوعي	usboo'eyy
weight (n)	وزن	wazn, awzaan
welcome (n)	ترحيب	tarHeeb
well (n, for water)	بئر	bi'r, aabaar
well done!	أحسنت!	aHsant
well done (cooking)	مطهو جيدا	maT-hoo jay-yidan
well-known (adj)	مشهور	mash-hoor
west	غرب	gharb
wet (adj)	مبتل	mubtall
what?	ماذا؟	maadha
wheat	قمح	qamH
wheel	عجلة	ajala, ajalaat
when?	متى؟	matta
where?	أين؟	aina
which?	أي؟	ayy
white	أبيض	abyaD

who?	من؟	*man*
whole (adj)	كامل	*kaamil*
wholesale	جملة	*jumla*
why?	لماذا؟	*limaazha*
wide	عريض	*'areeD*
widow	أرملة	*armala, araamil*
widower	أرمل	*armal, araamil*
wife	زوجة	*zawja, zawjaat*
wild (adj, reckless)	طائش	*Taa'ish*
wild (adj, uncultivated)	بري	*bar-reyy*
will (auxiliary verb)	سوف	*sawfa*
win (v, I)	يربح	*yarbaH*
wind (n)	ريح	*reeH, reeyaaH*
windmill	طاحونة	*TaaHoona, TawauHeen*
window	شباك	*shub-baak, shabaabeek*
windscreen	زجاج أمامي	*zujaaj amaameyy*
wine	نبيذ	*nabeedh*
wing (n)	جناح	*jinaaH, ajniHa*
winter	شتاء	*shitaa'*
wipe (v, I)	يمسح	*yamsaH*
wish (n)	أمنية	*umniya, umniyaat*
with (prep)	مع	*ma'*
withdraw (v, I)	يسحب	*yasHab*
woman	امرأة	*imra'a, nisaa'*

wood (n, timber)	خشب	khashab, akh-shaab
wool	صوف	Soof, aSwaaf
word	كلمة	kalima, kalimaat
work (n, job)	عمل	'amal
world	عالم	'aalam
worm	دودة	dooda, dood
worse	أسوأ	aswa'
worth (n)	قيمة	qeema
wound (n)	جرح	jarH, jiraaH
wreckage	حطام	HuTaam
write (v, I)	يكتب	yaktub
wrong (adj)	خاطئ	khaaTi'

X, Y, Z

x-ray	أشعة	ashi'aa
yacht	يخت	yakht, yukhoot
year	سنة	sana, sanawaat
yearly	سنوي	sanaweyy
yeast	خميرة	khameera
Yemen	اليمن	al-yaman
Yemeni	يمني	yamaneyy, yamaney-yeen
yesterday	أمس	ams
yogurt	زبادي	zabaadee

young (adj)	صغير السن	*sagheer as-sinn*
youth price	سعر الشباب	*s'ir ash-shabaab*
youth hostel	بيت الشباب	*bait ash-shabaab*
zebra	حمار وحشي	*Himaar waH-sheyy*
zero	صفر	*Sifr*
zest (n, lemon)	قشرة	*qishra*
zoo	حديقة الحيوان	*Hadeeqat al-Hayawaan*

ARABIC–ENGLISH DICTIONARY

The *Arabic–English Dictionary* is arranged in the order of the Arabic alphabet – see pages 8–9 for reference. Remember Arabic is read from right to left. For the purposes of this book the *pages* run in the English order (left-hand page followed by right-hand page).

Plurals of common words are given in transliteration after the singular, e.g. rabbit **arnab, araanib**.

Verbs are listed under the present tense, third person masculine ("he" form), e.g. **yaktub, yadrus**. Each verb is followed by a reference, e.g. **agree** (v, *III*). The roman numerals refer to the verb form (see page 188). Irregular verbs are also indicated, e.g. **add** (v, *I hollow*). Each type of irregular verb has tables for reference in the Appendix (pages 191–200).

You will also find a general introduction to Arabic verbs on page 188.

father (n) *ab*	أب
smile (n) *ibtisaama, ibtisaamaat*	ابتسامة
creativity *ibtikaar*	ابتكار
never; ever (adv) *abadan*	أبدا
son *ibn, abnaa'*	ابن
nephew (son of brother) *ibn akh*	ابن أخ
nephew (son of sister) *ibn ukht*	ابن أخت
daughter *ibna, banaat*	ابنة
paternal *abaweyy*	أبوي
parents *abawain*	أبوين
white *abyaD*	أبيض
monuments *aathaar*	آثار
relic *athar, aathaar*	أثر
couple (n) *ithnain*	اثنين
answer (n) *ijaaba, ijaabaat*	إجابة
obligatory; mandatory *ijbaareyy*	إجباري
charge (fee); wage (salary) *ajr, ujoor*	أجر
litigation *ijraa'aat qaDaa'ey-ya*	إجراءات قضائية
price, fare *ujra*	أجرة
foreigner *ajnabee*	أجنبي
caution (prudence) *iHtiraas*	احتراس
respect (n) *iHtiraam*	احترام
look out! *iHtaris!*	احترس!
celebration *iHtifaal, iHtifaalaat*	احتفال

possibility *iHtimaal*	احتمال
best *aHsan*	أحسن
well done! *aHsant*	أحسنت!
lipstick *aHmar shifaah*	أحمر شفاة
brother *akh, ukhwa*	أخ
sister *ukht, akhawaat*	أخت
test (n) *ikhtibaar, ikhtibaaraat*	اختبار
kidnap (n) *ikhtiTaaf*	اختطاف
choice *ikhtiyaar*	اختيار
optional *ikhti-yaareyy*	اختياري
other; another *aakhar*	آخر
last; ultimate (adj) *akheer*	أخير
administration; management *idaara*	إدارة
literature *adab*	أدب
ear *udhun, aadhaan*	أذن
appointment *irtibaaT, irtibaaTaat*	ارتباط
concussion *irtijaaj*	ارتجاج
altitude *irtifaa', irtifaa'aat*	ارتفاع
Jordanian *urdunneyy, urdunney-yeen*	أردني
land (n) *arD, araaDi*	أرض
floor (n) *arDey-ya*	أرضية
insomnia *araq*	أرق
widower *armal, araamil*	أرمل
widow *armala, araamil*	أرملة
rabbit *arnab, araanib*	أرنب
blue *azraq*	أزرق

azure **azraq samaaweyy**	أزرق سماوي
offence (n, insult) **isaa'a, isaa'aat**	إساءة
base (n, foundation) **asaas**	أساس
elementary (basic) **asaaseyy**	أساسي
week **usboo', asaabee'**	أسبوع
weekly **usboo'eyy**	أسبوعي
break (n, respite) **istiraaHa**	استراحة
consultant **istishaareyy**	استشاري
resignation **istiqaala**	استقالة
reception (n, hotel) **istiqbaal**	استقبال
Israel **israa-eel**	إسرائيل
Israeli **israa-eelee**	إسرائيلي
family **usra, usarr**	أسرة
dynasty (n) **usra Haakima**	أسرة حاكمة
legend (myth) **usToora, asaaTeer**	أسطورة
ambulance **is'aaf**	إسعاف
sorry **aasif**	آسف
below **asfal**	أسفل
ancestors **aslaaf**	أسلاف
Islamic **islaameyy**	إسلامي
name **ism, asmaa'**	اسم
diarrhea **is≠haal**	إسهال
shares (n) **ashum**	أسهم
worse **aswa'**	أسوأ
black (color) **aswad**	أسود
x-ray **ashi'aa**	أشعة

blonde (adj) *ashqar*	أشقر
left-handed *ashwal*	أشول
injury *iSaaba, iSaabaat*	إصابة
finger *iSba', aSaabi'*	إصبع
artificial *iSTinaa'eyy*	اصطناعي
bald *aSla'*	أصلع
original; genuine; authentic *aSleyy*	أصلي
deaf *aSamm*	أصم
thoroughbred *aSeel*	أصيل
extra *iDaafeyy*	إضافي
tire (n) *iTaar, iTaaraat*	إطار
limbs *aTraaf*	أطراف
ruins (n) *aTlaal*	أطلال
bachelor *a'zab, 'uzaab*	أعزب
advertising (n) *i'laan*	إعلان
above *a'la*	أعلى
blind (adj, without sight) *a'maa*	أعمى
majority *aghlabey-ya*	أغلبية
song *ughneya, aghaani*	أغنية
better *afDal*	أفضل
Afghanistan *afghaanistaan*	أفغانستان
Afghan (adj) *afghaani, afghaan*	أفغاني
landscape (adj, horizontal) *ufuqeyy*	أفقي
accommodation *iqaama*	إقامة
suggestion *iqtiraaH, iqtiraaHaat*	اقتراح
economic; budget (adj) *iqtiSaadeyy*	اقتصادي

next of kin *aqrab al-aqribaa'*	أقرب الأقرباء
maximum *aqSaa*	أقصى
less (adj, fewer); least (adj) *aqall*	أقل
province *iqleem, aqaaleem*	إقليم
regional *iqleemee*	إقليمي
more *akthar*	أكثر
tip (n, gratuity) *ikramey-ya, ikramey-yaat*	إكرامية
food *akl*	أكل
Jordan *al-urdunn*	الأردن
elder (n) *al-akbar*	الأكبر
Emirates *al-imaaraat*	الإمارات
labor pains *aalaam al-waD'*	آلام الوضع
United Nations *al-umam al-muttaHida*	الأمم المتحدة
now *al-aan*	الآن
instrument *aala, aalaat*	آلة
laryngitis *iltihaab al-hanjara*	التهاب الحنجرة
Algeria *al-jazaa'ir*	الجزائر
pilgrimage (to Mecca) *al-Hajj*	الحج
fall (n, season) *al-khareef*	الخريف
Casablanca *ad-daar al- bayDaa'*	الدار البيضاء
spring (n, season) *ar-rabee'*	الربيع
Saudi (Arabia) *as-sa'oodey-ya*	السعودية
Sudan *as-soodaan*	السودان
colloquial language *al-'aamey-ya*	العامية
Iraq *al-'iraaq*	العراق

	أم
Arabic language **al-'arabeyya**	العربية
cancellation **ilghaa'**	إلغاء
Euphrates **al-furaat**	الفرات
Cairo **al-qaahira**	القاهرة
Kabyle (in Algeria) **al-kabaa'il**	القبائل
Jerusalem **al-quds**	القدس
Koran **al-quraan al-kareem**	القرآن الكريم
alcohol **al-kuHool**	الكحول
earth (planet) **al-kura l-arDey-ya**	الكرة الأرضية
Kaaba (in Mecca) **al-kaa'ba**	الكعبة
Kuwait **al-kuwait**	الكويت
English language **al-lugha al-ingeleezey-ya**	اللغة الانجليزية
Allah; God **al-laah**	الله
tonight **al-laila**	الليلة
pain; ache (n) **alam, aalaam**	ألم
Christianity **al-maseeHey-ya**	المسيحية
Levant **al-mashriq al-'arabi**	المشرق العربي
Morocco **al-maghrib**	المغرب
Nubia **an-nooba**	النوبة
Nile **an-neel**	النيل
down(wards) **ila asfal**	إلى أسفل
until (prep) **ila 'an**	إلى أن
Yemen **al-yaman**	اليمن
today **al-yawm**	اليوم
mother (n) **umm**	أم

forward (adj) *amaameyy*	أمامي
examination (test) *imtiHaan, imtiHaanaat*	امتحان
baggage (n) *amti'a*	أمتعة
gratitude (adj) *imtinaan*	امتنان
excellence *imtiyaaz*	امتياز
woman *imra'a, nisaa'*	امرأة
gynecology *amraaD nisaa'*	أمراض نساء
yesterday *ams*	أمس
constipation *imsaak*	إمساك
security (n) *amn*	أمن
wish (n) *umnia, umniyaat*	أمنية
emir; prince *ameer, umaraa'*	أمير
princess *ameera, ameeraat*	أميرة
I *ana*	أنا
snorkel (n) *unboob at-tanaf-fus*	أنبوب التنفس
uprising *intifaaDa*	انتفاضة
female *untha*	أنثى
England *ingeltera*	انجلترا
English (person) *ingeleezeyy, ingeleez*	انجليزي
Bible *injeel*	انجيل
bend (n, contour) *inHinaa'*	انحناء
nose *anf*	أنف
rescue (n) *inqaadh*	إنقاذ
breakdown (n, nervous) *inhiyaar 'aSabeyy*	انهيار عصبي
insult (n) *ihaana, ihaanaat*	إهانة

باذ

or *aw*	أو
Europe *orob-baa*	أوروبا
European *orob-beyy, orob-bey-yeen*	أوروبي
sale (n, discount) *okazyon, okazyonaat*	أوكازيون
first *aw-wal*	أول
anybody *ayy shakhS*	أي شخص
anything *ayy shai'*	أي شيء
anywhere *ayy makaan*	أي مكان
which? *ayy*	أي؟
positive *eejaabee*	ايجابي
Iran *eeraan*	إيران
Iranian *eeraaneyy*	إيراني
receipt *eeSaal, eeSaalaat*	إيصال
also *aiDan*	أيضا
beat (n, tempo, music) *eeqaa'*	إيقاع
icon *ayqoona, ayqoonaat*	أيقونة
faith; belief *'eeman*	إيمان
where? *aina*	أين؟

ب (baa)

door *baab, abwaab*	باب
bus *baaS, baaSaat*	باص
Babylon *baabil*	بابل
eggplant *baadhinjaan*	باذنجان

well (n, for water) *bi'r, aabaar*	بئر
cold (adj) *baarid*	بارد
peas *bazilaa'*	بازلاء
coach (n, bus) *baaS, baaSaat*	باص
void (adj, invalidated) *baaTil*	باطل
mosquito *baa'ooDa, baa'ooD*	باعوضة
across *bil'arD*	بالعرض
okra *bamya*	بامية
veal *bitel-lo*	بتللو
beside *bijaanib*	بجانب
sailor *baH-Haar, baH-Haara*	بحار
sea *baHr*	بحر
marine (adj) *baHreyy*	بحري
Bahrain *al-baHrayn*	البحرين
Bahraini *baIIrayneyy*	بحريني
lake *buHaira, buHairaat*	بحيرة
incense (aromatic products) *bukhoor*	بخور
precisely *bi-diq-qa*	بدقة
instead of *badalan 'an*	بدلا عن
Bedouin *badaweyy*	بدوي
suit (n, clothing) *badhla*	بذلة
overland *bar-ran*	برا
Berber *barbar*	بربر
orange (n, fruit) *burtuqaala, burtuqaal*	برتقال
orange (adj, color) *burtuqaaleyy*	برتقالي
tower *burj, abraaj*	برج

lightning **barq**	برق
pool (n, pond, etc.) **birka, birak**	بركة
proof **burhaan**	برهان
wild (adj, uncultivated) **bar-reyy**	بري
innocent (adj, not guilty) **baree'**	بريء
mail (n, post) **bareed**	بريد
airmail (n) **bareed jaw-weyy**	بريد جوي
British (adj) **biriTaaneyy, biriTaaney-yeen**	بريطاني
Britain **biriTaanya**	بريطانيا
lozenge pastille **basteelya**	بستيلية
simple **baseeT**	بسيط
eyesight **baSar**	بصر
onion **baSal**	بصل
card **biTaaqa, biTaaqaat**	بطاقة
postcard **biTaqa bareedey-ya**	بطاقة بريدية
charge card **biTaaqat Hisaab**	بطاقة حساب
unemployment (n) **biTaala**	بطالة
blanket **baT-Taney-ya, baTaaTeen**	بطانية
duck (n) **baT-Ta, baTT**	بطة
slow (adj) **baTee'**	بطيء
after (prep) **ba'd**	بعد
afternoon (n) **ba'd aDH-DHuhr**	بعد الظهر
some **baa'D**	بعض
far **ba'eed**	بعيد
grocer **baq-qaal**	بقال

cow	**baqara, baqar**	بقرة
spot (n, stain)	**buq'a, buqa'**	بقعة
unattended	**bilaa riqaaba**	بلا رقابة
date (fruit)	**balaHa, balaH**	بلحة
bilingual	**bilughatain**	بلغتين
blouse	**bilooza**	بلوزة
coffee (beans)	**bunn**	بن
building	**binaa', abneya**	بناء
girl	**bint, banaat**	بنت
niece (daughter of brother)	**bint akh**	بنت أخ
niece (daughter of sister)	**bint ukht**	بنت أخت
gas (n, petrol)	**banzeen**	بنزين
purple	**banafsajeyy**	بنفسجي
lavender (n, color)	**banafsajeyy faatiH**	بنفسجي فاتح
brown	**bun-neyy**	بني
hall	**bahw**	بهو
gate	**baw-waaba, baw-waabaat**	بوابة
inch	**booSa, booSaat**	بوصة
environment	**bee'a**	بيئة
linen	**bayaDaat**	بياضات
breakdown (n, itemization)	**bayaan mufaS-Sal**	بيان مفصل
home; house	**bait, buyoot**	بيت
youth hostel	**bait ash-shabaab**	بيت الشباب
kennel	**bayt al-kalb, buyoot al-kilaab**	بيت الكلب
mansion	**bait fakhm, buyoot fakhma**	بيت فخم

تحف

Bethlehem **bait laHm**	بيت لحم
beer **beera**	بيرة
bureaucracy **beeroqraTey-ya**	بيروقراطية
egg **baiDa, baiD**	بيضة
veterinary **baiTareyy**	بيطري
between **bain**	بين

(taa) ت

sarcophagus **taaboot Hajareyy**	تابوت حجري
trader **taajir, tuj-jaar**	تاجر
date (day); history **taareekh, tawaareekh**	تاريخ
visa **ta'sheera, ta'sheeraat**	تأشيرة
cab (n) **taksee**	تاكسي
next **taali**	تال
total (adj, entire) **taam**	تام
insurance **ta'meen**	تأمين
restoration **tajdeed**	تجديد
manicure **tajmeel aDHaafir al-yad**	تجميل أظافر اليد
cavity **tajweef**	تجويف
under (prep) **taHt**	تحت
caution (n, warning) **taHdheer**	تحذير
antiques **tuHaf qadeema**	تحف قديمة
masterpiece **tuHfa, tuHaf**	تحفة

embalming (n) *taHneeT*	تحنيط
transfer (n) *taHweel, taHweelaat*	تحويل
greeting (n) *taHey-ya, taHey-yaat*	تحية
camping trip (n) *takhyeem*	تخييم
massage *tadleek*	تدليك
memento *tidhkaar*	تذكار
ticket (n) *tadhkara, tadhaakir*	تذكرة
taste (n, sense) *tadhaw-wuq*	تذوق
dust (n) *turaab*	تراب
consent (n) *taraaDi*	تراض
welcome (n) *tarHeeb*	ترحيب
license *tarkheeS, taraakheeS*	ترخيص
tailor (n) *tarzi, tarzey-ya*	ترزي
upgrade (n) *tarqeya*	ترقية
Turkey *torkeya*	تركيا
lubrication *tazyeet*	تزييت
climb (n) *tasal-luq*	تسلق
entertainment *tasliya*	تسلية
marketing *tasweeq*	تسويق
similarity *tashaabuh*	تشابه
diagnosis *tash-kheeS*	تشخيص
trim (n, hair, etc.) *tash-dheeb*	تشذيب
assortment *tashkeela*	تشكيلة
crash (n) *taSaadum*	تصادم
pass (n, permit) *taSreeH, taSaareeH*	تصريح
repair (n) *taSleeH*	تصليح

	نهم
vaccination; inoculation **taT'eem**	تطعيم
voluntary (n) **tataw-wu'eyy**	تطوعي
tired (adj) **ta'baan**	تعبان
expression (phrase) **ta'beer, ta'beeraat**	تعبير
breakdown (n, malfunction) **Ta'aT-Tul**	تعطل
education **ta'leem**	تعليم
compensation **ta'weeD**	تعويض
miserable (sad) **ta'ees**	تعيس
change (n, alteration) **taghyeer,** **taghyeeraat**	تغيير
apple **tufaaHa, tufaaH**	تفاحة
details **tafaaSeel**	تفاصيل
retirement (from work) **taqaa'ud**	تقاعد
customs (n, traditions) **taqaaleed**	تقاليد
estimate (n) **taqdeer**	تقدير
almost **taqreeban**	تقريبا
traditional (adj) **taqleedeyy**	تقليدي
air conditioning (n) **takyeef ul-hawaa'**	تكييف الهواء
hill **tall, tilaal**	تل
damage (n) **talaf**	تلف
statue **timthaal, tamaatheel**	تمثال
exercise (n) **tamreen, tamreenaat**	تمرين
crocodile **timsaaH, tamaaseeH**	تمساح
excavation **tanqeeb**	تنقيب
leak (n) **tanqeeT**	تنقيط
charge (n, accusation) **tuhma**	تهمة

ventilation *tahwiya*	تهوية
spices (n) *tawaabil*	توابل
dressing (n, salad flavoring) *tawaabil as-salaTa*	توابل السلطة
twin *taw'am, tawaa'im*	توأم
recommendation *tawSey-ya*	توصية
signature *tawqee', tawqee'aat*	توقيع
Tunis *toonis*	تونس
Tunisian *tooniseyy, toonisey-yeen*	تونسي
current (electric) *tay-yaar kahrubaa'eyy*	تيار كهربائي
current (water) *tay-yaar maa'eyy*	تيار مائي
fig *teena, teen*	تينة

ث (thaa)

second (n, after first) *thaani*	ثان
second (n, time) *thaanya, thawaani*	ثانية
chit-chat (n) *tharthara*	ثرثرة
hole; puncture *thuqb, thuqoob*	ثقب
keyhole *thuqb al-moftaaH*	ثقب المفتاح
heavy *thaqeel*	ثقيل
fridge *thal-laaja, thal-laajaat*	ثلاجة
ice *thalj*	ثلج
cost (n) *thaman*	ثمن
valuable *thameen*	ثمين

جري

garlic **thawm** ثوم

ج (jeem)

dry (adj) **jaaf**	جاف
gallon **galoon**	جالون
university **jaami'a, jaami'aat**	جامعة
buffalo **jaamoosa, jaamoos**	جاموسة
ready (adj) **jaahiz**	جاهز
mountain **jabal, jibaal**	جبل
cheese **jubna**	جبنة
grandfather **jidd**	جد
serious **jid-deyy**	جدي
new **jadeed**	جديد
attractive **jadh-dhaab**	جذاب
root (n) **jidhr, judhoor**	جذر
germs **jaraatheem**	جراثيم
surgery (n, operation) **jiraaHa, jiraaHaat**	جراحة
wound (n) **jarH, jiraaH**	جرح
rat **jurdh, jurdhaan**	جرذ
doorbell **jaras al-baab**	جرس الباب
waiter (n) **garsoon**	جرسون
dosage **jur'a, jur'aat**	جرعة
newspaper **jareeda, jaraa'id**	جريدة
crime **jareema, jaraa'im**	جريمة

part (n, section) *juz', ajzaa'*	جزء
Algerian *jazaa'ireyy, jazaa'irey-yeen*	جزائري
butcher (n) *jaz-zaar, jaz-zaareen*	جزار
carrot *jazar*	جزر
island *jazeera, juzur*	جزيرة
bridge (n) *jisr, jusoor*	جسر
body *jism, ajsaam*	جسم
skin (n); leather *jild*	جلد
customs (n, import duties) *jamaarik*	جمارك
shrimp; prawns *gambari (coll.)*	جمبري
camel *jamal, jimaal*	جمل
wholesale *jumla*	جملة
beautiful *jameel*	جميل
wing (n); suite (hotel) *jinaaH, ajniHa*	جناح
soldier (n) *jundeyy, junood*	جندي
ginger (n, herb) *ganzabeel*	جنزبيل
nationality *jinsey-ya, jinsey-yaat*	جنسية
appliance *jihaaz, ajhiza*	جهاز
effort *juhd, juhood*	جهد
weather (n) *jaww*	جو
passport *jawaaz safar*	جواز سفر
guava *jawaafa*	جوافة
quality (n) *jawda*	جودة
hunger (n) *joo'*	جوع
excursion; tour (n) *jawla, jawlaaat*	جولة
cruise (n) *jawla baHrey-ya*	جولة بحرية

	حبه
skirt **gunel-la, gunel-laat**	جونلة
gem **jawhara, jawaahir**	جوهرة
jeweler **jawharjeyy**	جوهرجي
pocket (n) **jaib, juyoob**	جيب
skirt **jeeba, jeebaat**	جيبة

(Haa) ح

wall **Haa'iT, Hawaa'iT**	حائط
Wailing Wall **Haa'iT al-mabka**	حائط المبكى
pilgrim **Haajj, Hujjaaj**	حاج
eyebrow **Haajib, Hawaajib**	حاجب
need (n) **Haaja, Haajaat**	حاجة
rabbi **Haakhaam**	حاخام
accident **Haadith, Hawaadith**	حادث
hot **Harr**	حار
guard (n); keeper (of park, etc.) **Haaris, Hor-ras**	حارس
hoof **Haafir, Hawaafir**	حافر
wallet **HaafiDHa**	حافظة
case; condition (n) **Haala**	حالة
pregnant **Haamil**	حامل
love (n) **Hubb**	حب
rope **Habl, Hibaal**	حبل
cardamom **Hab-bahaan**	حبهان

breakfast cereal **Huboob al-fuToor**	حبوب الفطور
veil (n) **Hijaab**	حجاب
stone (n) **Hajar, aHjaar**	حجر
room (n, hotel, etc.) **Hujra, Hujraat**	حجرة
reservation (n) **Hajz, Hujuzaat**	حجز
size (n) **Hajm, aHjaam**	حجم
edge; limit **Hadd, Hudood**	حد
minimum charge **Hadd adnaa**	حد أدنى
iron (n, metal) **Hadeed**	حديد
garden; park (n) **Hadeeqa, Hadaa'iq**	حديقة
zoo **Hadeeqat al-Hayawaan**	حديقة الحيوان
shoe **Hidhaa', aHdheya**	حذاء
dialing tone **Haraara**	حرارة (تليفون)
war **Harb**	حرب
letter (alphabet) **Harf, Huroof**	حرف
craftsmanship **Hirafey-ya**	حرفية
sunburn (n) **Hurooq ash-shams**	حروق الشمس
silk (n) **Hareer**	حرير
silk (adj) **Hareereyy**	حريري
party (n, political group) **Hizb, aHzaab**	حزب
Labor Party **Hizb al-'ummaal**	حزب العمال
unhappy; sad **Hazeen**	حزين
account (n, bank) **Hisaab, Hisaabaat**	حساب
current account **Hisaab jaari**	حساب جار
allergic; sensitive **Has-saas**	حساس
good **Hasan**	حسن

	حما
insect *Hashra, Hashraat*	حشرة
horse *HiSaan, aHSina*	حصان
measles *HaSba*	حصبة
civilization *HaDaara, HaDaaraat*	حضارة
wreckage *HuTaam*	حطام
luck *HaDH*	حظ
diaper *Haf-faaDa*	حفاضة
party (n, ball) *Hafla, Haflaat*	حفلة
concert (n) *Hafla museeqey-ya*	حفلة موسيقية
grandchild *Hafeed, aHfaad*	حفيد
right (n, entitlement) *Haqq, Huqooq*	حق
syringe (n); jab *Huqna, Huqan*	حقنة
bag (n) *Haqeeba, Haqaa'ib*	حقيبة
handbag *Haqeebat yad*	حقيبة يد
fact *Haqeeqa, Haqaa'iq*	حقيقة
real; true *Haqeeqeyy*	حقيقي
itching *Hak-ka*	حكة
solution (n, answer) *Hall, Hulool*	حل
compromise (n) *Hall wasaT*	حل وسط
barber *Hal-laaq, Hal-laaqeen*	حلاق
dream (n) *Hilm, aHlaam*	حلم
sweet (adj) *Hulw*	حلو
candy *Halwaa*	حلوى
milk *Haleeb*	حليب
donkey *Himaar, Hameer*	حمار
zebra *Himaar waH-sheyy*	حمار وحشي

porter *Ham-maal, Ham-maaleen*	حمال
bathroom *Ham-maam*	حمام
chickpeas *Hum-muS*	حمص
lamb (young sheep) *Hamal*	حمل
load (n) *Himl, aHmaal*	حمل
father-in-law *Hamw*	حمو
acidity *HumooDa*	حموضة
fever *Hum-maa*	حمى
henna *Henaa'*	حناء
faucet *Hanafey-ya, Hanafey-yaat*	حنفية
sink (n) *HawD, aHwaaD*	حوض
around *Hawl*	حول
alive; live (adj, wire, etc.) *Hayy*	حي
commercial district *Hayy tijaareyy*	حي تجاري
life *Hayaa*	حياة
animal *Hayawaan, Hayawaanaat*	حيوان

خ (khaa)

afraid *khaa'if*	خائف
maid *khadima, khadimaat*	خادمة
exterior *khaarijeyy*	خارجي
private *khaaS*	خاص
equestrian (adj) *khaaS bil-furoosey-ya*	خاص بالفروسية
wrong (adj) *khaaTi'*	خاطئ

	خط
uncle (maternal) *khaal, khilaan*	خال
aunt (maternal) *khaala, khaalaat*	خالة
lean (adj, meat, etc.) *khaali ad-dihin*	خالي الدهن
news *khabar, akhbaar*	خبر
experience (n) *khibra, khibraat*	خبرة
bread *khubz*	خبز
circumcision *khitaan*	ختان
service (n, favor) *khidma, khidmaat*	خدمة
khedive *khudaywee*	خديوي
myth *khuraafa, khurafaat*	خرافة
junk *khurda*	خردة
knick-knacks *khurdawaat*	خردوات
artichoke *kharshoof (coll.)*	خرشوف
graduate (adj) *khir-reej*	خريج
map *khareeTa, kharaa'iT*	خريطة
closet *khazaanat malaabis*	خزانة ملابس
safe (n, secure box) *khazna, khizan*	خزنة
lettuce *khass*	خس
loss *khusaara*	خسارة
wood (n, timber) *khashab, akh-shaab*	خشب
beech (wood) *khashab az-zaan*	خشب الزان
rough (adj, not smooth) *khashin*	خشن
waist *khaSr*	خصر
rebate; discount (n) *khaSm, khuSumaat*	خصم
vegetable(s) *khuDaar*	خضار
line *khaTT, khuTooT*	خط

route (n) *khaTT sair*	خط سير
error *khaTa', akhTaa'*	خطأ
letter (mail) *khiTaab*	خطاب
hazard *khaTar*	خطر
dangerous *khaTir*	خطر
engagement (n, for marriage) *khuTooba*	خطوبة
step (n) *khaTwa, khaTwaat*	خطوة
fiancé (male) *khaTeeb*	خطيب
fiancée (female) *khaTeeba*	خطيبة
critical (adj, dangerous) *khaTeer*	خطير
light (adj, opp. heavy); mild *khafeef*	خفيف
vinegar *khall*	خل
during (prep); through (prep) *khilaal*	خلال
bangle *khal-khaal, khalaa-kheel*	خلخال
extraction (n, tooth, etc.) *khal'*	خلع
behind *khalf*	خلف
back (adj, rear) *khalfeyy*	خلفي
fault (n) *khalal*	خلل
gulf *khaleej*	خليج
blend; mixture *khaleeT*	خليط
caliph *khaleefa, kholafaa'*	خليفة
yeast *khameera*	خميرة
dagger *khanjar, khanaajir*	خنجر
fear (n) *khawf*	خوف
cucumber *khiyaar*	خيار
bamboo (n) *khaizaraan*	خيزران

درف

canvas **khaish**	خيش
string (cord) **khaiT, khuyooT**	خيط
tent **khaima, khiyaam**	خيمة

د *(daal)*

kleptomania **daa' as-sirqa**	داء السرقة
circle (n) **daa'ira, dawaa'ir**	دائرة
constant **daa'im**	دائم
always **daa'iman**	دائما
inside **daakhil**	داخل
interior (adj) **daakhileyy**	داخلي
house **daar, diyaar**	دار
warm (adj) **daafi'**	دافئ
hornet **dab-boor, dabaabeer**	دبور
pin (n) **dab-boos, dabaabees**	دبوس
chicken **dajaaj**	دجاج
impostor **daj-jaal, daj-jaaleen**	دجال
smoke (n) **dokh-khaan**	دخان
intruder **dakheel, dukhalaa'**	دخيل
bicycle **dar-raaja, dar-raajaat**	دراجة
degree; extent **daraja, darajaat**	درجة
temperature **darajat al-Haraara**	درجة الحرارة
lesson **dars, duroos**	درس
dolphin **darfeel, daraafeel**	درفيل

dervish **darweesh, daraaweesh**	درويش
dozen **dasta**	دستة
shower (n) **dush**	دش
flour **daqeeq**	دقيق
minute (n, time) **daqeeqa, daqaa'iq**	دقيقة
guidebook **daleel**	دليل
manual (n, booklet) **daleel maTboo'**	دليل مطبوع
blood (n) **dam**	دم
Damascus **dimashq**	دمشق
tear (n, drop) **dam'a, dumoo'**	دمعة
doll **dumya, dumyaat**	دمية
lace (n) **dantella**	دنتلة
fat (n) **duhn**	دهن
medicine; drug **dawaa', adweya-**	دواء
worm **dooda, dood**	دودة
carafe **dawraq, dawaariq**	دورق
country (n, state) **dawla**	دولة
international **duwaleyy**	دولي
monastery, abbey **dair, adyira**	دير
turkey **deek roomeyy**	ديك رومي
religion **deen, adyaan**	دين

ذ *(dhaal)*

same (adj) **dhaatuh**	ذاته

رحا

fly (n, insect) **dhobaaba, dhobaab**	ذبابة
arm (n, anatomical) **dhiraa'**	ذراع
maize **Dhur-ra**	ذرة
male **dhakar, dhukoor**	ذكر
memories **dhikrayaat**	ذكريات
round-trip **dhihaab wa 'awda**	ذهاب وعودة
gold (n) **dhahab**	ذهب

ر (raay)

smell (n, scent) **raa'iHa, rawaa'iH**	رائحة
terrific **raa'i**	رائع
lung **ri'a**	رئة
head (n, anatomy) **ra's, ru'oos**	رأس
adult **raashid, raashideen**	راشد
passenger **raakib, ruk-kaab**	راكب
view (n, opinion) **ra'yy, aaraa'**	رأي
main (adj, central) **ra'eeseyy**	رئيسي
shoelace **ribaaT al-hizhaa'**	رباط الحذاء
quarter (n) **rub'**	ربع
maybe **rub-bama**	ربما
asthma **rabu**	ربو
man **rajul, rijaal**	رجل
leg **rijl, arjul**	رجل
nomad **raH'Haal**	رحال

journey; trip (n, voyage) **riHla, riHlaaat**	رحلة
flight (n, air journey) **riHlat Tayaraan**	رحلة طيران
departure **raHeel**	رحيل
marble (n, stone) **rukhaam**	رخام
inexpensive; cheap **rakheeS**	رخيص
reply (n) **radd, rudood**	رد
rice **ruzz**	رز
message **risaala**	رسالة
formal (adj) **rasmee**	رسمي
prophet **rasool**	رسول
grace (n, elegance) **rashaaqa**	رشاقة
Rosetta **rasheed**	رشيد
lead (n, metal) **ruSaaS**	رصاص
platform (n, for train) **raSeef, arSifa**	رصيف
satisfaction **riDaa**	رضا
humidity **ruTooba**	رطوبة
lather **raghwa**	رغوة
loaf (n, bread) **ragheef, arghifa**	رغيف
companion **rafeeq, rifaaq**	رفيق
neck **raqba**	رقبة
number **raqm, arqaam**	رقم
delicate **raqeeq**	رقيق
knee **rukba, rukab**	ركبة
corner (n) **rukn, arkaan**	ركن
riding (n) **rukoob al-khail**	ركوب الخيل
cycling **rukoob ad-dar-raajaat**	ركوب الدراجات

pomegranate *rum-maan*	رمان
eyelash *rimsh, rumoosh*	رمش
Ramadan *ramaDaan*	رمضان
sand (n) *raml, rimaal*	رمل
bet (n) *rahaan, rahaanaat*	رهان
prescription *rooshet-ta*	روشتة
kindergarten *rawDat aTfaal*	روضة أطفال
khamsin winds *riyaaH al-khamaaseen*	رياح الخماسين
sport (n) *riyaaDa*	رياضة
athletic *riyaaDeyy*	رياضي
mathematics *riyaaDiyaat*	رياضيات
wind (n) *reeH, reeyaaH*	ريح
basil *reeHaan*	ريحان
countryside *reef*	ريف
provincial; rustic *reefeyy*	ريفي

(zaay) ز

angle (n) *zaawiya, zawaayaa*	زاوية
yogurt *zabaadee*	زبادي
trash (n); litter *zibaala*	زبالة
butter *zubd*	زبد
client *zuboon, zabaa'in*	زبون
raisin *zibeeb*	زبيب
glass (n, for mirrors, etc.) *zujaaj*	زجاج

windscreen *zujaaj amaameyy*	زجاج أمامي
bottle *zujaaja, zujaajaat*	زجاجة
ornamental *zukhrufi*	زخرفي
button (n) *zirr*	زر
agriculture (n) *ziraa'a*	زراعة
thyme *za'tar*	زعتر
saffron *za'faraan*	زعفران
down (n, feathers) *zaghab*	زغب
wedding (n) *zifaaf*	زفاف
emerald (n) *zumur-rud*	زمرد
time (n, eras, etc.) *zaman*	زمن
rose *zahra, zuhoor*	زهرة
marriage *zawaaj*	زواج
husband *zawj, azwaaj*	زوج
wife *zawja, zawjaat*	زوجة
throat *zawr*	زور
launch (n, motorboat) *zawraq saree'*	زورق سريع
visit (n) *ziyaara, ziyaaraat*	زيارة
oil *zait, zuyoot*	زيت
olive *zaitoona, zaitoon*	زيتونة

س (seen)

misunderstanding *soo' fahm*	سوء فهم
tourist (n) *saa'iH, suyaaH*	سائح

driver *saa'iq, saa'iqeen*	سائق
liquid *saa'il, sawaa'il*	سائل
question (n) *su'aal, as'ila*	سؤال
coast (n, shore) *saaHil, sawaaHil*	ساحل
hour *saa'a, sa'aat*	ساعة
watch (n, on wrist) *saa'at yad*	ساعة يد
calm (adj) *saakin*	ساكن
bygone *saalif*	سالف
race (n, running, etc.) *sibaaq, sibaaqaat*	سباق
plumber *sab-baak*	سباك
reason; cause (n) *sabab, asbaab*	سبب
rosary *sibHa*	سبحة
curtain; screen *sitaar*	ستار
carpet (n); rug *sij-jaada, sij-jaad*	سجادة
mat *sij-jaada Sagheera*	سجادة صغيرة
sausage *sujuq*	سجق
prison; jail (n) *sijn, sujoon*	سجن
lizard *siHliyya, saHaali*	سحلية
heat (n) *sukhoona*	سخونة
dam *sadd, sudood*	سد
plug (n) *sad-daada*	سدادة
secret (n); mystery *sirr, asraar*	سر
mirage *saraab*	سراب
saddle (n) *sarj*	سرج
catacomb *sirdaab, saraadeeb*	سرداب
speed (n) *sur'a*	سرعة

burglary **sariqa, sariqaat**	سرقة
joy **suroor**	سرور
secret (adj) **sir-reyy**	سري
bed **sareer, asir-ra**	سرير
quick; fast **saree'**	سريع
inflammable **saree' l-ishti'aal**	سريع الاشتعال
cough (n) **su'aal**	سعال
price (n) **si'r, as'aar**	سعر
youth price **s'ir ash-shabaab**	سعر الشباب
Saudi (Arabian) **sa'oodeyy, sa'oodey-yeen**	سعودي
happy **sa'eed**	سعيد
embassy **sifaara, sifaaraat**	سفارة
ambassador **safeer, sufaraa'**	سفير
ship (n) **safeena, sufun**	سفينة
ceiling; roof **saqf, suqoof**	سقف
railroad **sikka Hadeed**	سكة حديد
sugar (n) **suk-kar**	سكر
intoxicated (adj) **sakraan, sakaara**	سكران
residential **sakaneyy**	سكني
knife (n) **sik-keen, sakaakeen**	سكين
breed (n) **sulaala, sulaalaat**	سلالة
peace **salaam**	سلام
basket **sal-la**	سلة
sultan **sulTaan**	سلطان
cable (n) **silk, aslaak**	سلك

سيف

ladder **sil-lim, salaalim**	سلم
descendant **saleel**	سليل
sky **samaa', samawaat**	سماء
broker **simsaar, samaasira**	سمسار
fish (n) **samak**	سمك
shark **samakat al-qirsh**	سمكة القرش
thick **sameek**	سميك
age (n) **sinn**	سن
hump (n, camel's back) **sanaam**	سنام
year **sana, sanawaat**	سنة
tooth **sin-na, asnaan**	سنة
yearly **sanaweyy**	سنوي
oversight **sahw**	سهو
bracelet **siwaar**	سوار
Sudanese **soodaaneyy, soodaaney-yeen**	سوداني
Syrian **sureyy, surey-yeen**	سوري
Syria **surey-yaa**	سوريا
fly (n, zipper) **sosta, sosat**	سوستة
will (auxiliary verb) **sawfa**	سوف
market (n) **sooq, aswaaq**	سوق
shopping mall **sooq mol**	سوق مول
vulgar **sooqeyy**	سوقي
unlucky (adj) **say-yi' al-HaDH**	سيء الحظ
car; vehicle **say-yaara, say-yaaraat**	سيارة
lady **sayyeda, sayyedaat**	سيدة
flush (n, toilet) **seefon**	سيفون

ش (sheen)

pale (adj) **shaaHib**	شاحب
truck (n); lorry **shaaHina, shaaHinaat**	شاحنة
beach **shaaTi', shawaaTi'**	شاطئ
thankful (adj) **shaakir**	شاكر
current affairs **shu'oon as-saa'a**	شؤون الساعة
tea (n) **shaay**	شاي
window **shub-baak, shabaabeek**	شباك
slippers **shibshib, shabaashib**	شبشب
web **shabaka**	شبكة
retina **shabakey-ya**	شبكية
winter **shitaa'**	شتاء
tree **shajara, ashjaar**	شجرة
cedar (n) **shajarat al-arz**	شجرة الأرز
shipment (n) **shuHna, shuHnaat**	شحنة
person **shakhS, ash-khaaS**	شخص
sail (n) **shiraa'**	شراع
condition (n, stipulation) **sharT, shurooT**	شرط
balcony; terrace **shurfa, shurfaat**	شرفة
east (n) **sharq**	شرق
eastern; oriental **sharqeyy**	شرقي
company (n, business unit) **sharika, sharikaat**	شركة
bay **sharm**	شرم

sunrise *shorooq*	شروق
artery *shiryaan, sharaayeen*	شريان
slice (n) *shareeHa, sharaa'iH*	شريحة
partner (n) *shareek, shurakaa'*	شريك
coral *shi'aab marjaaney-ya*	شعاب مرجانية
popular *sha'bee*	شعبي
hair *sha'r*	شعر
malt *sha'eer*	شعير
lip *shifaah*	شفاه
verbal *shafaweyy*	شفوي
apartment *shiq-qa, shuqaq*	شقة
doubt (n) *shakk*	شك
shape (n) *shakl, ashkaal*	شكل
waterfall *shal-laal, shal-laalaat*	شلال
smell (n, sense) *shamm*	شم
north *shamaal*	شمال
melon *sham-maam*	شمام
sun (n) *shams*	شمس
wax (n) *sham'*	شمع
candle *sham'a, shimoo'*	شمعة
university degree *shihaada jaame'ey-ya*	شهادة جامعية
month *shahr, shuhoor*	شهر
monthly *shahreyy*	شهري
gallant *shahm*	شهم
soup *shorba*	شوربة
fork *shawka, shuwak*	شوكة

شيء

thing *shai', ashyaa'*	شيء
sheik *shaikh, shuyookh*	شيخ
hookah; water pipe *sheesha*	شيشة
devil *shayTaan, shayaaTeen*	شيطان
blank check *sheek 'ala bayaaD*	شيك على بياض
traveler's checks *sheekaat seyaaHey-ya*	شيكات سياحية
rye (n) *shailam*	شيلم

ص (Saad)

soap (n) *Saaboon*	صابون
clear (adj, unclouded) *Saafi*	صاف
hotel lobby *Saalat al-funduq*	صالة الفندق
valid *SaaliH*	صالح
locksmith *Saani' aqfaal*	صانع أقفال
morning *SabaaH*	صباح
cactus *Sab-baar*	صبار
patience (n) *Sabr*	صبر
juvenile (adj) *Sibyaaneyy*	صبياني
press (n, magazines, etc.) *SaHaafa*	صحافة
journalist *SaHaafeyy, SaHafey-yeen*	صحافي
health *SiH-Ha*	صحة
desert (n) *SaHraa'*	صحراء،
reporter *SaHafee, SaHafeeyeen*	صحفي
plate (n, dish) *saHn, SuHoon*	صحن

صوف

sanitary *SiH-Heyy*	صحي
right (correct) *saHeeH*	صحيح
rock *Sakhra, Sokhoor*	صخرة
reef *Sukhoor baHrey-ya*	صخور بحرية
headache *Sodaa'*	صداع
migraine *Sudaa' niSfeyy*	صداع نصفي
breast *Sadr, Sudoor*	صدر
chance *Sudfa*	صدفة
charity (n, donation) *Sadaqa, Sadaqaat*	صدقة
shock (n) *Sadma, Sadmaat*	صدمة
friend *Sadeeq, aSdiqaa'*	صديق
epilepsy (n) *Sara'*	صرع
frank (honest) *SareeH*	صريح
difficult *Sa'b*	صعب
little; small *Sagheer*	صغير
young (adj) *sagheer as-sinn*	صغير السن
page (of a book, etc.) *SafHa, SafaHaat*	صفحة
zero *Sifr*	صفر
hepatitis *Safraa'*	صفراء
bargain (n) *Safqa, Safqaat*	صفقة
falcon; hawk *Saqr, Suqoor*	صقر
cross (n, crucifix) *Saleeb*	صليب
silence (n) *Samt*	صمت
sound (n); voice (n) *Sawt, aSwaat*	صوت
picture (n, photo, etc.) *Soora, Suwar*	صورة
wool *Soof, aSwaaf*	صوف

fast (n) *Sawm*	صوم
Lent *Siyaam al-maseeHey-yeen*	صيام المسيحيين
maintenance (servicing) *Siyaana*	صيانة
pharmacy *Saydaley-ya, Saydaley-yaat*	صيدلية
summer *Saif*	صيف

ض (Daad)

officer (military) *DaabiT, Dub-baaT*	ضابط
lamb (meat) *Daanee Sagheer*	ضاني صغير
fog *Dabaab*	ضباب
noise *Dajeej*	ضجيج
laughter *DaHik*	ضحك
massive *Dakhm*	ضخم
against *Didd*	ضد
knock out (n, boxing) *Darba qaaDey-ya*	ضربة قاضية
harm (n) *Darar*	ضرر
essential; necessary *Darooreyy*	ضروري
tax (n) *Dareeba, Daraa'ib*	ضريبة
mausoleum; shrine *DareeH, aDreHa*	ضريح
weak *Da'eef*	ضعيف
credit (n); warranty *Damaan*	ضمان
light (n, sunlight, etc.) *Daw', aDwaa'*	ضوء

طبي

headlights *Daw' 'aali*	ضوء، عال
guest (n) *Daif, Duyoof*	ضيف
narrow; tight *Day-yiq*	ضيق
company (n, guests) *Duyoof*	ضيوف

ط *(Taa)*

bird *Taa'ir, Tiyoor*	طائر
airplane *Taa'ira, Taa'iraat*	طائرة
wild (adj, reckless) *Taa'ish*	طائش
stamp (n, postage) *Taabi' bareed*	طابع بريد
story (n, level) *Taabiq, Tawaabiq*	طابق
windmill *TaaHoona, TawaaHeen*	طاحونة
repellent (n) *Taarid*	طارد
fresh *Taazij*	طازج
student (n) *Taalib, Talaba*	طالب
undergraduate *Taalib fee l-jaami'a*	طالب في الجامعة
backgammon *Tawlit az-zahr*	طاولة الزهر
cook (n, chef) *Tab-baakh, Tab-baakheen*	طباخ
dish (n) *Tabaq, aTbaaq*	طبق
dessert *Tabaq al-Hilw*	طبق الحلو
layer (n) *Tabaqa, Tabaqaat*	طبقة
medical *Tib-beyy*	طبي
dentist *Tabeeb asnaan*	طبيب أسنان

natural **Tabi'eyy**	طبيعي
style (n); make (n, brand, etc.) **Tiraaz, Tiraazaat**	طراز
fez **Tarboosh**	طربوش
package (n) **Tard, Turood**	طرد
soft **Tareyy**	طري
quaint **Tareef**	طريف
road; way (n, route) **Tareeq, Turuq**	طريق
cul-de-sac **Tareeq masdood**	طريق مسدود
way (n, method) **Tareeqa, Turuq**	طريقة
rash (n) **TafH jildee**	طفح جلدي
child; infant **Tifl, aTfaal**	طفل
parasite **Tofaileyy**	طفيلي
set (n, specific group) **Taqm, aTqum**brand	طقم
dentures **Taqm asnaan**	طقم أسنان
divorce (n) **Talaaq**	طلاق
request (n) **Talab, Talabaat**	طلب
loose (adj, free) **Taleeq**	طليق
tomato **TamaaTim**	طماطم
emergency (n) **Tawaari'**	طوارئ
lifebuoy **Tawq an-najaah, atwaaq an-najaah**	طوق النجاة
length **Tool**	طول
long (adj, lengthy) **Taweel**	طويل
kind (adj, good-natured) **Tay-yib**	طيب

عدس

ظ (DHaa)

shade (n, from sun, etc.) **DHil, DHilaal**	ظل
back (n, anatomical) **DHahr, DHuhoor**	ظهر

ع ('ain)

ivory **'aaj**	عاج
fair (just) **'aadil**	عادل
just (adj, fair) **'aadil**	عادل
exhaust (n, fumes) **'aadim**	عادم
normal; ordinary **'aadeyy**	عادي
condom **'aazil Tib-beyy, 'awaazil Tib-bey-ya**	عازل طبي
storm (n) **'aaSifa, 'awaaSif**	عاصفة
capital (city) **'aaSima, 'awaaSim**	عاصمة
high (tall) **aali**	عال
world **'aalam**	عالم
loud **'aali aS-Sawt**	عالي الصوت
ancient **'ateeq**	عتيق
disability **'ajz**	عجز
wheel **ajala, ajalaat**	عجلة
dough **'ajeen**	عجين
justice (n) **'adaala**	عدالة
lentils **'ads**	عدس

lens *adasa, adasaat*	عدسة
excuse (n) *'udhr, a'dhaar*	عذر
Iraqi *'iraaqeyy, iraaqey-yeen*	عراقي
Arab(ian) *'arabee*	عربي
performance; show (n); offer (n) *'arD, 'urooD*	عرض
bride *'aroosa, 'araa'is*	عروسة
bridegroom *'arees, 'irsaan*	عريس
wide *'areeD*	عريض
indigestion *'usr haDm*	عسر هضم
military (adj) *'askaree*	عسكري
honey *'asal*	عسل
dinner *'ashaa'*	عشاء
herb *'ushb, a'shaab*	عشب
nerve *'aSab, a'Saab*	عصب
modern *'aSree*	عصري
muscle *'aDala, 'aDalaat*	عضلة
organic *'uDwee*	عضوي
membership (n) *'uDwey-ya*	عضوية
thirsty *'atshaan*	عطشان
vacation; holiday; leave (n) *'uTla, 'uTlaat*	عطلة
bone *'aDHma, 'iDHaam*	عظمة
great (adj, marvelous) *'aDHeem*	عظيم
pardon (n, amnesty) *'afw*	عفو
knot *'uqda*	عقدة

عوا

carnelian **'aqeeq aHmar**	عقيق أحمر
reverse (n); opposite **'aks**	عكس
therapy; remedy; cure (n) **'ilaaj**	علاج
relationship **'ilaaqa, 'ilaaqaat**	علاقة
sign (n, mark) **'alaama, 'alaamaat**	علامة
box (n) **'ulba, 'ulab**	علبة
match-box **ulbat kibreet**	علبة كبريت
Egyptology **'ilm al-miSrey-yaat**	علم المصريات
on **'ala**	على
uncle (paternal) **'amm, 'amaam**	عم
Oman **'umaan**	عمان
Omani **'umaaneyy, umaaney-yeen**	عماني
aunt (paternal) **'am-ma, am-maat**	عمة
mayor **'umda, 'umad**	عمدة
work (n, job) **'amal**	عمل
currency **'umla, 'umlaat**	عملة
operation **'amaley-ya, 'amaley-yaat**	عملية
commission (fee) **'umoola, 'umoolaat**	عمولة
deep (adj) **'ameeq**	عميق
care (n) **'inaaya**	عناية
grape **'inaba, 'inab**	عنبة
ambergris **'anbar**	عنبر
ward (hospital) **'anbar, 'anaabir**	عنبر
goat **'anza, anzaat**	عنزة
address (n, street) **'unwaan, 'anaaween**	عنوان
rubber ring **'aw-waama**	عوامة

return (n) **'awda**	عودة
surgery (n, clinic) **'iyaada, 'iyaadaat**	عيادة
feast (n) **'eed, a'yaad**	عيد
Labor Day **'eed al-'ummaal**	عيد العمال
Easter **eed al-fiSH**	عيد الفصح
birthday **'eed milaad**	عيد ميلاد
eye (n, anatomical) **'ain, 'uyoon**	عين
sample (n, small example) **'ay-yina, 'ay-yinaat**	عينة

غ (ghain)

absent **ghaa'ib**	غائب
angry **ghaaDib**	غاضب
expensive **ghali**	غال
vague (adj) **ghaamiD**	غامض
tomorrow **ghadan**	غدا
lunch **ghadaa'**	غداء
gland **ghud-da, ghud-dad**	غدة
fine (n) **gharaama, gharaamaat**	غرامة
west **gharb**	غرب
vacancy (in hotel) **ghuraf khaaliya**	غرف خالية
theater (n, in hospital) **ghurfat al-'amaley-yaat**	غرفة العمليات
bedroom **ghurfat nawm**	غرفة نوم

غير

sunset	*ghoroob*	غروب
strange; funny (peculiar)	*ghareeb*	غريب
deer; gazelle	*ghazaal, ghuzlaan*	غزال
yarn (n, thread)	*ghazl*	غزل
dishwasher	*ghas-saalat aTbaaq*	غسالة أطباق
washing machine	*ghas-saalat malaabis*	غسالة ملابس
laundry (n, clothes, etc.)	*ghaseel*	غسيل
angry; cross	*ghaDbaan, ghaDbaaneen*	غضبان
cover (n, lid)	*ghaTaa', aghTey-ya*	غطاء
scuba diving (n)	*ghaTs*	غطس
kettle	*ghallaayat al-maa'*	غلاية الماء
mistake (n)	*ghalTa, ghalaTaat*	غلطة
wealthy	*ghaneyy*	غني
diving, scuba (n)	*ghawS*	غوص
unofficial	*ghair rasmeyy*	غير رسمي
unhealthy	*ghair SiH-Hi*	غير صحي
incorrect	*ghair saHeeH*	غير صحيح
unable	*ghair qaadir*	غير قادر
illegal	*ghair qaanooneyy*	غير قانوني
uncommon	*ghair ma'loof*	غير مألوف
uncomfortable	*ghair mureeH*	غير مريح
unreasonable	*ghair ma'qool*	غير معقول
unsuitable	*ghair munaasib*	غير مناسب
uncertain	*ghair waathiq*	غير واثق

ف *(faa)*

benefit (n); use (n) *faa'ida, fawaa'id*	فائدة
check (n, bill) *fatoora, fawaateer*	فاتورة
empty; blank *faarigh*	فارغ
bad, rotten *faasid*	فاسد
green beans *faSolya*	فاصوليا
indecent *faaDiH*	فاضح
fruit *faakiha, fawaakih*	فاكهة
lantern *fanoos, fawaanees*	فانوس
dawn (n) *fajr*	فجر
examination (n, medical) *faHS, fuHooSaat*	فحص
blood test *faHS dam*	فحص دم
pottery *fukh-khaar*	فخار
luxurious *fakhm*	فخم
strawberry *farawla*	فراولة
paradise *firdaws*	فردوس
mare *farasa, farasaat*	فرسة
opportunity *furSa, furaS*	فرصة
Pharaonic *fir'awneyy*	فرعوني
difference *farq, furooq*	فرق
oven *furn*	فرن
scalp (n) *farwat ar-ra's*	فروة الرأس
prey *fareesa*	فريسة

dress (n, clothing item) *fustaan, fasaateen*	فستان
season (n, spring, etc.) *faSl, fuSool*	فصل
blood group *faSeelat ad-dam*	فصيلة الدم
silver (n) *faD-Da*	فضة
silver (adj) *faD-Deyy*	فضي
breakfast *fuToor*	فطور
terrible *faDHee'*	فظيع
effective *fa'aal*	فعال
only; just *faqaT*	فقط
jaw *fakk*	فك
change (n, coins) *fak-ka*	فكة
idea *fikra, afkaar*	فكرة
Palestine *falasTeen*	فلسطين
Palestinian *falasTeeneyy, falasTeeney-yeen*	فلسطيني
pepper (n) *filfil*	فلفل
astronomical *falakeyy*	فلكي
mouth *fam*	فم
art *fann*	فن
calligraphy *fann al-khaTT*	فن الخط
lighthouse *fanaara*	فنارة
artist *fannaan, fannaaneen*	فنان
cup (n, for drinks) *finjaan, fanajeen*	فنجان
hotel *funduq, fanaadiq*	فندق
appetizers *fawaatiH ash-shahey-ya*	فواتح الشهية

immediate *fawreyy*	فوري
mess (n, chaos) *fawDa*	فوضى
up *fawq*	فوق
fava beans *fool*	فول
in *fee*	في
unconscious *fee ighmaa'a*	في إغماءة
outside *fil-khaarij*	في الخارج
elephant *feel, afyaal*	فيل
movie *film, aflaam*	فيلم

ق (qaaf)

leader (n, chief) *qaa'id, qaada*	قائد
menu; list (n) *qaa'ima, qawaa'im*	قائمة
lifeboat *qaarib an-najaah, qawaarib an-najaah*	قارب النجاة
magistrate *qaaDi aw-wal*	قاض أول
lounge (n) *qaa'at jiloos, qaa'aat jiloos*	قاعة جلوس
dictionary *qaamoos, qawaamees*	قاموس
law *qaanoon, qawaaneen*	قانون
legal *qanooneyy*	قانوني
dome *qub-ba, qibaab*	قبة
Copt (n) *qibTeyy, aqbaaT*	قبطي
hat *quba'a*	قبعة
before *qabl*	قبل

	قطر
kiss (n) *qubla, qublaat*	قبلة
tribe *qabeela, qabaa'il*	قبيلة
mass (church service) *qud-daas*	قداس
foot *qadam, aqdaam*	قدم
able *qadeer*	قدير
saint *qid-dees, qid-deeseen*	قديس
old (object) *qadeem*	قديم
dirty (adj) *qadhir*	قذر
ulcer *qurHa*	قرحة
pill *qurS, aqraaS*	قرص
tablet *qurS, aqraaS*	قرص
loan (n) *qarD, qurooD*	قرض
rural *qaraweyy*	قروي
near *qareeb*	قريب
relative (n) *qareeb, aqaarib*	قريب
village *qarya, quraa*	قرية
station (n, police) *qism al-bolees*	قسم البوليس
zest (n, lemon); plate (gold, etc.) *qishra*	قشرة
story (n, tale) *qiS-Sa, qiSaS*	قصة
palace *qaSr, quSoor*	قصر
short (adj, opp. long) *qaSeer*	قصير
case (n, court) *qaDey-ya*	قضية
train (n) *qiTaar, qiTaaraa*	قطار
cat *qiT-Ta, qiTaT*	قطة
Qatar *qaTar*	قطر
Qatari *qaTareyy, qaTarey-yeen*	قطري

piece (n) **qiT'a, qiTa'**	قطعة
cotton (n) **quTn**	قطن
velvet **qaTeefa**	قطيفة
leap (n) **qafza, qafzaat**	قفزة
lock (n); padlock (n) **qifl, aqfaal**	قفل
heart **qalb, quloob**	قلب
castle; citadel; fortress **qal'a, qilaa'**	قلعة
uneasy; concerned; worried **qaliq**	قلق
pencil **qalam ruSaaS**	قلم رصاص
few (adj) **qaleel**	قليل
gambling **qumaar**	قمار
fabric; material **qumaash, aqmisha**	قماش
wheat **qamH**	قمح
moon **qamar, aqmaar**	قمر
satellite **qamar Sinaa'eyy**	قمر صناعي
lunar **qamareyy**	قمري
shirt (n) **qameeS, qumSaan**	قميص
canal (n, channel) **qanaah, qanawaat**	قناة
mask (n) **qinaa', aqni'a**	قناع
jellyfish **qandeel al-baHr**	قنديل البحر
consulate **qunSuley-ya, qunSuley-yaat**	قنصلية
coffee (beverage) **qahwa**	قهوة
black coffee (no sugar) **qahwa saada**	قهوة سادة
strength **quw-wa, quw-waat**	قوة
strong **qaweyy**	قوي

كحل

measurement; fitting (n, trying on) **qiyaas**	قياس
worth (n) **qeema**	قيمة

ك (kaaf)

cabin (n) **kabeena, kabaa'in**	كابينة
untrue **kaadhib**	كاذب
phonecard **kart at-tilifon**	كارت التليفون
cup (n, trophy) **ka's, ku'oos**	كأس
khaki (n, color) **kaakee**	كاكي
full; perfect; whole **kaamil**	كامل
kebob **kabaab**	كباب
liver **kabid**	كبد
matches **kibreet**	كبريت
knob (n, of butter, etc.) **kabsha, kabshaat**	كبشة
big; large **kabeer**	كبير
book (n, novel, etc.) **kitaab, kutub**	كتاب
ketchup **kitshab**	كتشب
shoulder (n) **katif, aktaaf**	كتف
pamphlet **kutay-yib**	كتيب
many; plenty **katheer**	كثير
dense **katheef**	كثيف
kohl **koHl**	كحل

tie (n, neck) *karavatta*	كرافتة
ball (n) *kura, kuraat*	كرة
soccer *kurat al-qadam*	كرة القدم
Kurd *kurdeyy, akraad*	كردي
cherries *karz*	كرز
chair; seat (n) *kurseyy, karaasee*	كرسي
celery *karafs*	كرفس
hospitality *karam aD-Diyaafa*	كرم الضيافة
generous *kareem*	كريم
fracture (n) *kasr*	كسر
saucepan *kasarol-la*	كسرولة
lazy *kasool, kasaala*	كسول
kiosk *kushk, akshaak*	كشك
newsstand *kushk al-jaraa'id*	كشك الجرائد
palm (n, anatomy) *kaff*	كف
enough *kifaaya*	كفاية
all; each; every *kull*	كل
dog *kalb, kilaab*	كلب
word *kalima, kalimaat*	كلمة
kidney *kilya*	كلية
college *kul-ley-ya, kul-ley-yaat*	كلية
sleeve (n) *kumm, akmaam*	كم
quantity; amount *kam-mey-ya, kam-mey-yaat*	كمية
church *kaneesa, kanaa'is*	كنيسة
such *ka-haazha*	كهذا

electricity **kahrabaa'**	كهرباء
amber **kahramaan**	كهرمان
cave (n) **kahf, kuhoof**	كهف
hairdresser **kewafeer**	كوافير
glass (n, tumbler, etc.) **koob, akwaab**	كوب
elbow **koo', akwaa'**	كوع
tights **kolonaat**	كولونات
Kuwaiti **kuwaiteyy, kuwaitey-yeen**	كويتي
pillow case **kees wisaada**	كيس وسادة
how **kaif**	كيف
kilogram **keelograam**	كيلوجرام
kilometer **keelomitr**	كيلومتر
chemistry **keemyaa'**	كيمياء

(laam) ل

nobody **laa aHad**	لا أحد
nothing **laa shai'**	لا شئ
unbelievable **laa yuSad-daq**	لا يصدق
unbearable **laa yuTaaq**	لا يطاق
sign (n, display board) **laafita, laafitaat**	لافتة
pearl **lu'lu'a, lu'lu'**	لؤلؤة
because **la'ann**	لأن
lavender (n, plant) **lawanda**	لاونده
Lebanon **lubnaan**	لبنان

Lebanese *lubnaaneyy, lubnaaney-yeen*	لبناني
liter *litr*	لتر
moment *laHdha, laHdhaat*	لحظة
meat *laHm*	لحم
beef *laHm baqareyy*	لحم بقري
beard *liHya, liHaa*	لحية
tongue *lisaan, alsina*	لسان
thief (n) *liSS, luSooS*	لص
curse (n, evil spell) *la'na*	لعنة
language *lugha, lughaat*	لغة
why? *limaazha*	لماذا؟
ours *lina*	لنا
dialect; accent (n, speech) *lahja, lahjaat*	لهجة
if *lau*	لو
beans, runner *lubya*	لوبيا
lotus *lootos*	لوتس
keyboard (computer, etc.) *lawHat mafaateeH*	لوحة مفاتيح
almonds *lawz*	لوز
loofah *loofa*	لوفة
color (n) *lawn, alwaan*	لون
Libyan *leebeyy, leebey-yeen*	ليبي
Libya *leebya*	ليبيا
night *lail, layaali*	ليل
lime (citrus fruit) *laymoon akhDar*	ليمون أخضر
lemon *laymoon aSfar*	ليمون أصفر

lemonade *laymoonada*	ليمونادة

م *(meem)*

except *maa 'adaa*	ما عدا
beyond *maa waraa'*	ما وراء
water (n) *maa'*	ماء
table (n) *maa'ida, mawaa'id*	مائدة
polite *mu'ad-dab*	مؤدب
what? *maadha*	ماذا؟
muezzin *mu'adh-dhin,* *mu'adh-dhineen*	مؤذن
minaret *mi'dhana, ma'aadhin*	مئذنة
March *maaris*	مارس
Maronite *maarooneyy, marooney-yeen*	ماروني
diamonds *maas*	ماس
past (adj) *maaDi*	ماض
temporary *mu'aq-qat*	مؤقت
money *maal*	مال
author (n) *mu'al-lif, mu'al-lifeen*	مؤلف
owner *maalik*	مالك
common (adj, familiar) *ma'loof*	مألوف
safe (adj, opp. risky) *ma'moon*	مأمون
mango *mango*	مانجو
exchange (n) *mubaadala*	مبادلة

match (n, sport) *mubaaraah*	مباراة
straight; direct (adj, non-stop) *mubaashir*	مباشر
wet (adj) *mubtall*	مبتل
early *mubak-kir*	مبكر
terminal (n, airport) *mabna al-maTaar*	مبنى المطار
late *muta'akh-khir*	متأخر
trouble (n) *mataa'ib*	متاعب
museum *matHaf, mataaHif*	متحف
translator; interpreter *mutarjim, mutarjimeen*	مترجم
undecided *mutarad-did*	متردد
even (adj, levelled) *mutasaawi*	متساو
volunteer (n) *mutaTaw-wi', mutaTaw-wi'een*	متطوع
advanced (adj) *mutaqad-dim*	متقدم
unstable *mutaqal-lib*	متقلب
contradictory *mutanaaqiD*	متناقض
mobile *mutanaq-qil*	متنقل
wild (adj, savage) *mutawaH-Hish*	متوحش
average; central; medium *mutawas-siT*	متوسط
available *mutawaf-fir*	متوفر
when? *matta*	متى؟
example *mithaal, amthila*	مثال
bladder *mathaana*	مثانة

محل

cultured (erudite) *muthaq-qaf, muthaq-qafeen* — مثقف

like (similar to) *mithl* — مثل

triangle *muthal-lath, muthal-lathaat* — مثلث

risk (n) *mujaazafa, mujaazafaat* — مجازفة

complimentary; free (adj, gratis) *maj-jaaneyy* — مجاني

criminal (n) *mujrim, mujrimeen* — مجرم

magazine (periodical) *majal-la, majal-laat* — مجلة

frozen (adj) *mujam-mad* — مجمد

sum; total *majmoo'* — مجموع

group (n) *majmoo'a, majmoo'aat* — مجموعة

mad (crazy) *majnoon, majaaneen* — مجنون

unknown (adj) *majhool* — مجهول

accountant *muHaasib, muHaasibeen* — محاسب

lecture (n) *muHaadara, muHaadaraat* — محاضرة

attorney; lawyer *muHaami, moHaami-yeen* — محام

professional *muHtarif, muHtarifeen* — محترف

inevitable *maHtoom* — محتوم

engine *muHar-rik, muHar-rikaat* — محرك

station (n) *maHaT-Ta, maHaT-Taat* — محطة

lucky *maH-DHooDH* — محظوظ

store (n); shop (n) *maHal, maHal-laat* — محل

florist **maHall ward**	محل ورد
solution (n, liquid) **maHlool**	محلول
magnesium milk **maHlool al-magneezya**	محلول المجنيزيا
local **maHal-leyy**	محلي
ocean **muHeeT, muHeeTaat**	محيط
brain **mukh**	مخ
bakery **makhbaz, makhaabiz**	مخبز
crazy **makhbool**	مخبول
drug (narcotic) **mukhad-dir, mukhad-diraat**	مخدر
exit (n) **makhraj, makhaarij**	مخرج
beaten (adj, whisked) **makhfooq**	مخفوق
entrance **madkhal, madaakhil**	مدخل
coach (n, trainer) **mudar-rib, mudar-ribeen**	مدرب
amphitheatre **mudar-raj**	مدرج
school (n) **madrasa, madaaris**	مدرسة
heater **midfa'a**	مدفأة
urban (adj) **madaneyy**	مدني
director (n, senior executive) **mudeer**	مدير
city; town **madeena, mudun**	مدينة
flavor **madhaaq**	مذاق
masculine **mudhakkar**	مذكر
marvelous **mudh-hil**	مذهل
mirror **mir'aah, miraayaat**	مرآة

adolescent; teenager *muraahiq, muraahiqeen*	مراهق
square (n) *muraba', murab-ba'aat*	مربع
check (adj, pattern) *murab-ba'aat*	مربعات
jam (n) *murab-baa*	مربى
marmalade *murabba al-burtuqaal*	مربى البرتقال
once *mar-ra*	مرة
again (adv) *marra ukhra*	مرة أخرى
mattress *martaba, maraatib*	مرتبة
margarine *marjareen*	مرجرين
disease *maraD, amraaD*	مرض
diabetes *maraD as-suk-kar*	مرض السكر
refreshments *muraT-Tibaat*	مرطبات
boat *markib, maraakib*	مركب
central (adj, main) *markazeyy*	مركزي
exhausted *murhaq*	مرهق
fan (n, cooling) *marwaHa, maraawiH*	مروحة
traffic (n, cars, etc.) *muroor*	مرور
comfortable *mureeH*	مريح
ill; sick (person) *mareeD, marDaa*	مريض
auction (n) *mazaad, mazaadaat*	مزاد
double (adj) *muzdawaj*	مزدوج
farm (n) *mazra'a, mazaari'*	مزرعة
nuisance (adj) *muz'ij*	مزعج
chronic *muzmin*	مزمن

fake (adj) *muzayyaf*	مزيف
evening *masaa'*	مساء
help (n) *musaa'ida*	مساعدة
distance (n) *masaafa*	مسافة
equal (adj) *musawi*	مساو
responsible; in charge *mas'ool*	مسؤول
tenant (n) *musta'jir, musta'jireen*	مستأجر
impossible *mustaHeel*	مستحيل
round (adj, spherical) *mustadeer*	مستدير
orientalist *mustashriq, mustashriqeen*	مستشرق
hospital *mustashfa*	مستشفى
rectangle *mustaTeel, mustaTeelaat*	مستطيل
future (n) *mustaqbal*	مستقبل
independent *musta-qill*	مستقل
imported (adj) *mustawrad*	مستورد
level (n, water, etc.) *mustawa,* *mustawayaat*	مستوى
mosque *masjid, masaajid*	مسجد
powder (adj); powder (n) *masHooq,* *masaaHeeq*	مسحوق
theater (n, plays) *masraH, masaariH*	مسرح
play (n) *masraHey-ya, masraHey-yaat*	مسرحية
flat (adj, opp. bumpy) *musaT-TaH*	مسطح
mascara *maskaara*	مسكارا
sedative *musak-kin, musak-kinaat*	مسكن
obelisk *misal-la, misal-laat*	مسلة

مطلب

elderly; old (person) *musinn, musin-neen* مسن

Christian *maseeHeyy, maseeHey-yeen* مسيحي

lattice window *mashrabeyya, mashrabey-yaat* مشربية

drink (n) *mashroob, mashroobaat* مشروب

liquor *mashroobaat rawHey-ya* مشروبات روحية

busy (adj) *mash-ghool* مشغول

problem *mushkila, mashaakil* مشكلة

apricot *mishmish* مشمش

famous; well-known *mash-hoor* مشهور

expenses *maSaareef* مصاريف

lamp *miSbaaH, maSaabeeH* مصباح

Egypt *miSr* مصر

Egyptian *misreyy, miSrey-yeen* مصري

elevator *miS'ad, maSaa'id* مصعد

factory *maSna', maSaani'* مصنع

photographer *muSaw-wir, muSaw-wireen* مصور

exact *maDbooT* مضبوط

funny (humorous) *muD-Hik* مضحك

stewardess *maDeefa, maDeefaat* مضيفة

identical *muTaabiq* مطابق

airport *maTaar, maTaaraat* مطار

kitchen *maTbakh, maTaabikh* مطبخ

press (n, printing) *maTba'a, maTaabi'* مطبعة

rain (n) *maTar*	مطر
embroidered *moTar-raz*	مطرز
mallet *miTraqa khashabey-ya*	مطرقة خشبية
beaten (adj, frequented) *maTrooq*	مطروق
restaurant *maT'am, maTaa'im*	مطعم
antiseptic (adj) *muTah-hir*	مطهر
well done (cooking) *maT-hoo jay-yidan*	مطهو جيدا
envelope *maDHroof, maDHaareef*	مظروف
umbrella *miDHal-la, miDHal-laat*	مظلة
dark (unlit) *muDHlim*	مظلم
look (n, appearance) *maDHar, maDHaahir*	مظهر
with (prep) *ma'*	مع
down river *ma' majraa an-nahr*	مع مجرى النهر
together (adj) *ma'an*	معا
disabled (n) *mu'aaq*	معاق
landmarks *ma'aalim*	معالم
temple *ma'bad, ma'aabid*	معبد
moderate (adj) *mu'tadil*	معتدل
infectious; contagious *mu'di*	معد
stomach (n) *ma'ida*	معدة
rate (n) *mu'ad-dal*	معدل
metal *ma'dan*	معدن
ferry (n) *mi'ad-dey-ya*	معدية
gallery; exhibition *ma'raD, ma'aariD*	معرض
exempt *ma'fi*	معفي

reasonable *ma'qool*	معقول
teacher *mu'al-lim, mu'al-limeen*	معلم
information *ma'loomaat*	معلومات
architect *mi'maareyy*	معماري
laboratory *ma'mal, ma'aamil*	معمل
meaning *ma'naa*	معنى
gastric; intestinal *ma'aweyy*	معوي
imperfect *ma'eeb*	ميب
adventure *mughaamara, mughaamaraat*	مغامرة
Moroccan *maghribeyy, maghaariba*	مغربي
ladle *maghrafa, maghaarif*	مغرفة
vain *maghroor*	مغرور
laundry (n, facility) *maghsala*	مغسلة
closed *mughlaq*	مغلق
unexpected (adj) *mufaaji'*	مفاجئ
surprise (n) *mufaaja'a, mufaaja'aat*	مفاجأة
key *muftaaH, mafaateeH*	مفتاح
open (adj) *maftooH*	مفتوح
mufti *mufti*	مفتي
missing *mafqood, mafqoodeen*	مفقود
useful *mufeed*	مفيد
tomb *maqbara, maqaabir*	مقبرة
knob (n, door handle, etc.) *miqbaD, maqaabiD*	مقبض
holy; sacred *muqad-das*	مقدس

down payment *muqad-dam*	مقدم
skim (adj, milk) *maqshood*	مقشود
imitation (adj, copied) *muqal-lad*	مقلد
brakes *makaabiH*	مكابح
treat (n); reward (n) *mukaafa'a*	مكافأة
call (n, a phonecall) *mukaalama,*	مكالمة
mukaalamaat	
place (n, location) *makaan, amaakin*	مكان
lodging *makaan iqaama*	مكان إقامة
Mecca *makka*	مكة
office *maktab, makaatib*	مكتب
post office *maktab al-bareed*	مكتب البريد
bureau de change *maktab Sar-raaf*	مكتب صراف
bookshop; library *maktaba, maktabaat*	مكتبة
macaroni *makarona*	مكرونة
nuts (n, walnuts, etc.) *mukas-saraat*	مكسرات
ingredients *mukaw-winaat*	مكونات
make-up (n, lipstick, etc.) *mikyaaj*	مكياج
sheet *milaa'a, milaa'aat*	ملاءة
clothes *malaabis*	ملابس
malaria *malarya*	ملاريا
sore *multahib*	ملتهب
salt (n) *malH, amlaaH*	ملح
spoon (n) *mil'aqa, malaa'iq*	ملعقة
king *malik, muluuk*	ملك
queen *malika, malikaat*	ملكة

laxative *mulay-yin, mulay-yinaat*	ملين
path *mamarr*	ممر
nurse *mumar-riDa, momar-riDaat*	ممرضة
boring (adj, tedious) *mumill*	ممل
kingdom *mamlaka, mamaalik*	مملكة
forbidden; prohibited *mamnoo'*	ممنوع
deadly; fatal; lethal *mumeet*	مميت
who? *man*	من؟
convenient; suitable; fitting *munaasib*	مناسب
occasion *munaasaba, munaasabaat*	مناسبة
dairy products *muntajaat al-albaan*	منتجات الألبان
resort (n) *muntaja', muntaja'aat*	منتجع
midnight *muntaSaf al-lail*	منتصف الليل
low *munkhafiD*	منخفض
representative (n) *mandoob, mandoobeen*	مندوب
salesman *mandoob mabee'aat*	مندوب مبيعات
handkerchief *mindeel*	منديل
towel *minshafa, manaashif*	منشفة
logic *manTiq*	منطق
landscape; scenery *manDHar, manaaDHir*	منظر
detergent *munaDH-DHif, munaDH-DHifaat*	منظف
charity (n) *munaDH-DHama khairey-ya*	منظمة خيرية

alone *munfarid*	منفرد
separately *munfaSileen*	منفصلين
engraved (adj) *manqoosh*	منقوش
skill (n) *mahaara, mahaaraat*	مهارة
filly *muhra*	مهرة
festival *mahrajaan*	مهرجان
important *muhimm*	مهم
engineer *muhandis, muhandiseen*	مهندس
reliable *mawthooq bih*	موثوق به
wave (n, in sea) *mawja, amwaaj*	موجة
banana *mawza, mawz*	موزة
razor *moos Hilaaqa*	موس حلاقة
music *museeqa*	موسيقى
fashion *moDa*	موضة
subject (n, topic) *mawDoo',* *mawDoo'aat*	موضوع
habitat *mawTin*	موطن
employee *muwaDH-DHaf,* *muwaDH-DHafeen*	موظف
appointment; date *maw'id, mawaa'eed*	موعد
stand (n, position) *mawqif, mawaaqif*	موقف
terminal (n, bus) *mawqaf al-otobees*	موقف الأوتوبيس
mummy *mumya'a, mumyawaat*	مومياء
mineral water *miyaah ma'daney-ya*	مياه معدنية
balance (n, scales) *meezaan*	ميزان
budget (n, fiscal) *meezaney-ya*	ميزانية

mechanic *mekaneeki* ميكانيكي

harbor; port *meena', mawaani'* ميناء،

ن *(noon)*

asleep *naa'im* نائم

lively *naabiD* نابض

side (n) *naaHiya, nawaaHi* ناحية

unusual; rare *naadir* نادر

fire (n, flame) *naar* نار

people *naas* ناس

smooth (adj) *naa'im* ناعم

fountain *nafoora, nafooraat* نافورة

plant (n) *nabaat, nabaataat* نبات

vegetarian *nabaateyy* نباتي

wine *nabeedh* نبيذ

result (n) *nateeja, nataa'ij* نتيجة

carpenter *naj-jaar, naj-jaareen* نجار

star (n) *nijm, nujoom* نجم

brass *naHaas aSfar* نحاس أصفر

misfortune (bad luck) *naHs* نحس

bee *naHla, naHl* نحلة

towards (prep) *naHwa* نحو

thin *naHeef* نحيف

marrow *nukhaa'* نخاع

palm tree *nakhla, nakhl*	نخلة
eagle *nisr, nisoor*	نسر
textile *naseej*	نسيج
tapestry *naseej muzakhraf*	نسيج مزخرف
activity *nashaaT, anshiTa*	نشاط
energetic *nasheeT*	نشيط
crook *naS-Saab, naS-Saabeen*	نصاب
half *niSf, anSaaf*	نصف
advice (n) *naSeeHa, naSaa'iH*	نصيحة
optician *naDH-DHaraati*	نظاراتي
glasses *naDH-DHaara*	نظارة
system; order (n, method) *niDHaam, anDHima*	نظام
diet *niDHaam tagh-dheya*	نظام تغذية
clean (adj) *naDHeef*	نظيف
mint (n, herb) *ni'naa'*	نعناع
tunnel (n) *nafaq, anfaaq*	نفق
precious *nafees*	نفيس
stretcher *naq-qaala*	نقالة
point (n, dot) *nuqTa, nuqaTT*	نقطة
blood transfusion *naql dam*	نقل دم
pure *naqeyy*	نقي
final *nihaa'i*	نهائي
end (n) *nihaaya*	نهاية
seizure (n, fit) *nawba, nawbaat*	نوبة
Nubian *noobeyy, noobey-yeen*	نوبي

واد

type (n) *naw', anwaa'*	نوع
raw *nayy'*	نيء

ه *(haa)*

quiet (adj) *haadi'*	هادئ
gift *hadey-ya, hadaaya*	هدية
this *haadha*	هذا
pyramid *haram, ahraam*	هرم
fragile *hash-sh*	هش
crescent *hilaal*	هلال
panic (n) *hala'*	هلع
here *huna*	هنا
there *Hunaak*	هناك
air (n) *hawaa'*	هواء
hobby *huwaaya, huwayaat*	هواية
hieroglyphic *heeroghleefee*	هيروغليفي

و *(waaw)*

sure *waathiq*	واثق
duty (n, obligation) *waajib, waajibaat*	واجب
oasis *waaHa, waaHaat*	واحة
valley *waadi, widyaan*	واد

واس

loose (adj, baggy) **waasi'**	واسع
obvious; clear (adj, unambiguous) **waaDiH**	واضح
meal **wajba, wajbaat**	وجبة
face (n, anatomy) **wajh, wujooh**	وجه
destination **wijha, wijhaat**	وجهة
lonely **waHeed**	وحيد
amicable **wid-deyy**	ودي
hereditary **wiraathy**	وراثي
flower (n, rose, etc.) **warda, ward**	وردة
paper (n, sheet, etc.) **waraq, awraaq**	ورق
papyrus **waraq al-bardi**	ورق البردي
bay leaves **waraq al-ghaar**	ورق الغار
leaf **waraqat shajar, awraaq shajar**	ورقة شجر
lump; inflammation **waram, awraam**	ورم
vein (anatomy) **wareed, awrida**	وريد
weight (n) **wazn, awzaan**	وزن
middle **waSaT**	وسط
amid **wasT**	وسط
transportation **waseelat tanaq-qul**	وسيلة تنقل
handsome **waseem**	وسيم
recipe **waSfa, waSfaat**	وصفة
link **waSla, waSlaat**	وصلة
arrival **wuSool**	وصول
guardian **waSeyy**	وصي

vacancy (job opportunity) *waDHaa'if khaaliya*	وظائف خالية
job *waDHeefa, waDHaa'if*	وظيفة
promise (n) *wa'd, wu'ood*	وعد
loyal; faithful *wafeyy*	وفي
kneepad *wiqaa' ar-rukba*	وقاء الركبة
time (n, of day) *waqt*	وقت
fuel (n) *waqood*	وقود
agency (n) *wikaala, wikaalaat*	وكالة
birth (n) *wilaada, wilaadaat*	ولادة
United States *al-wilaayaat al-muttaHida*	الولايات المتحدة
boy *walad, awlaad*	ولد
unreal *wahmeyy*	وهمي

(yaa) ي

come (v, I defective) *ya'tee*	يأتي
hire; lease; rent (v, II) *yu'aj-jir*	يؤجر
take (v, I) *ya'khudh*	يأخذ
regret (v, I) *ya'saf*	يأسف
jasmine *yasmeen*	ياسمين
ruby (n) *yaaqoot*	ياقوت
confirm (v, II) *yu'ak-kid*	يؤكد
eat (v, I) *ya'kul*	يأكل

hurt (v, *IV*) **yu'lim**	يؤلم
order (v, *I*; demand) **ya'mur**	يأمر
hope (v, *I*) **ya'mal**	يأمل
exchange (v, *III*) **yubaadil**	يبادل
search (v, *I*) **yabHath**	يبحث
start; begin (v, *I*) **yabda'**	يبدأ
remove (v, *IV*) **yub'id**	يبعد
stay; remain (v, *I defective*) **yabqa**	يبقى
cry (v, *I defective*; weep) **yabkee**	يبكي
swallow (v, *I*; ingest) **yabla'**	يبلع
inform (v, *II*) **yubal-ligh**	يبلغ
sell (v, *I hollow*) **yabee'**	يبيع
follow (v, *I*) **yatba'**	يتبع
marinade; season (v, *II*) **yutab-bil**	يتبل
exceed (v, *VI*) **yatajaawaz**	يتجاوز
head (v, *VIII assimilated*; move towards) **yat-tajih**	يتجه
tour (v, *V*; visit) **yatajaw-wal**	يتجول
move (v, *V*) **yataHar-rak**	يتحرك
train (v, *V*) **yatadar-rab**	يتدرب
remember (v, *V*) **yatadhak-kar**	يتذكر
leave (v, *I*; abandon) **yatruk**	يترك
marry (v, *V*) **yatazaw-waj**	يتزوج
climb (v, *V*) **yatasal-laq**	يتسلق
shop (v, *V*) **yatasaw-waq**	يتسوق
quarrel (v, *VI*) **yatashaajar**	يتشاجر

يحس

call (v, *VIII assimilated*; phone) **yat-taSil**   يتصل

imagine (v, *V*) **yataSaw-war**   يتصور

tire (v, *I*) **yat'ab**   يتعب

trip (v, *V*; stumble) **yata'ath-thar**   يتعثر

learn (v, *V*) **yata'allam**   يتعلم

vomit (v, *V*) **yataqay-ya'**   يتقيأ

talk; speak (v, *V*) **yatakal-lam**   يتكلم

expect (v, *V*) **yatawaq-qa'**   يتوقع

trust (v, *I assimilated*) **yathiq**   يثق

pierce (v, *I*) **yathqub**   يثقب

find (v, *I assimilated*) **yajid**   يجد

draw (v, *I*) **yajdhub**   يجذب

tow (v); draw (v, *I doubled*) **yajurr**   يجر

sample (v, *II*; try) **yujar-rib**   يجرب

run (v, *I defective*; jog) **yajree**   يجري

sit (v, *I*) **yajlis**   يجلس

try (v, *III*) **yuHaawil**   يحاول

love; like (v, *IV doubled*) **yuHibb**   يحب

need (v, *VIII hollow*) **yaHtaaj**   يحتاج

keep (v, *VIII*; retain) **yaHtafiDH**   يحتفظ

reserve; book (v, *I*) **yaHjiz**   يحجز

happen (v, *I*) **yaHduth**   يحدث

burn (v, *I*) **yaHriq**   يحرق

pack (v, *I*) **yaHzim**   يحزم

calculate (v, *I*) **yaHsib**   يحسب

improve (v, *II*) **yuHas-sin**	يحسن
obtain (v, *I*) **yaHSul 'alaa**	يحصل على
inject (v, *I*) **yaHqin**	يحقن
resolve (v, *I doubled*) **yaHill**	يحل
shave (v, *I*) **yaHlaq**	يحلق
dream (v, *I*) **yaHlam**	يحلم
carry (v, *I*) **yaHmil**	يحمل
long (v, *I doubled*; miss) **yaHinn**	يحن
turn (v, *II*; transform) **yuHaw-wil**	يحول
fear (v, *I hollow*) **yakhaaf min**	يخاف من
tell (v, *IV*) **yukhbir**	يخبر
yacht **yakht, yukhoot**	يخت
select; choose (v, *VIII hollow*) **yakhtaar**	يختار
vanish (v, *V VIII defective*) **yakhtafee**	يختفي
direct (v, *IV*; a movie, etc..) **yukhrIj**	يخرج
deduct (v, *I*) **yakhSim**	يخصم
vacate (v, *IV defective*) **yukhlee**	يخلي
hand (n, anatomy) **yad, ayaadi**	يد
save (v, *II*; set aside) **yad-dakhir**	يدخر
enter (v, *I*) **yadkhol**	يدخل
smoke (v, *II*) **yudakh-khin**	يدخن
gossip (v, *I*) **yudardish**	يدردش
study (v, *I*) **yadrus**	يدرس
invite (v, *I defective*) **yad'oo**	يدعو
push; pay (v, *I*) **yadfa'**	يدفع
direct (v, *I doubled*; guide) **yadull**	يدل

manual (adj, by hand) **yadaweyy**	يدوي
run (v, I hollow; operate) **yudeer**	يدير
owe (v, I hollow) **yadeen**	يدين
go (v, I) **yadh-hab**	يذهب
melt; dissolve (v, I hollow) **yadhoob**	يذوب
watch (v, III; observe) **yuraaqib**	يراقب
win (v, I) **yarbaH**	يربح
tie (v, I) **yarbuT**	يربط
breed (v, II defective) **yurab-bee**	يربي
arrange (v, II) **yurat-tib**	يرتب
rise (v, VIII) **yartafi'**	يرتفع
reply (v, I doubled) **yarudd**	يرد
send (v, IV) **yursil**	يرسل
mail (v, IV; letters) **yursil bil-bareed**	يرسل بالبريد
draw (v, I; illustrate) **yarsim**	يرسم
refuse (v, I) **yarfuD**	يرفض
raise (v, I) **yarfa'**	يرفع
dance (v, I) **yarquS**	يرقص
kneel (v, I) **yarka'**	يركع
throw (v, I defective) **yarmee**	يرمي
see (v, I defective) **yara**	يرى
want (v, IV hollow) **yureed**	يريد
plant (v, I) **yazra'**	يزرع
increase (v, I hollow) **yazeed**	يزيد
left (opp. right) **yasaar**	يسار
help (v, III) **yusaa'id**	يساعد

travel (v, III) **yusaafir**	يسافر
ask (v, I) **yas'al**	يسأل
back (v, III; support) **yusaanid**	يساند
haggle (v, III) **yusaawim**	يساوم
swim (v, I) **yasbaH**	يسبح
relax (v, VIII) **yastajim**	يستجم
use (v, X) **yastakhdim**	يستخدم
rest (v, X hollow) **yastareeH**	يستريح
explore (v, X) **yastakshif**	يستكشف
receive (v, VIII) **yastalim**	يستلم
enjoy (v, X) **yastamti'**	يستمتع
listen (v, VIII) **yastami'**	يستمع
wake (v, X) **yastaiqiDH**	يستيقظ
pull (v, I) **yasHab**	يسحب
settle (v, II) **yusad-did**	يسدد
hurry; rush (v, I) **yusri'**	يسرع
fall (v, I; tumble) **yasquT**	يسقط
live (v, I; dwell) **yaskun**	يسكن
allow; permit (v, I) **yasmaH**	يسمح
market (v, II) **yusaw-wiq**	يسوق
buy (v, VIII defective) **yashtaree**	يشتري
curse (v, I; abuse verbally) **yashtim**	يشتم
charge (v, I; fill up) **yash-Hin**	يشحن
drink (v, I) **yashrib**	يشرب
explain (v, I) **yashraH**	يشرح
feel (v, I) **yash'ur**	يشعر

يضع

recover (v, *I defective*) **yushfa**   يشفى

complain (v, *I defective*) **yashkoo**   يشكو

smell (v, *I doubled*) **yashimm**   يشم

include (v, *I*) **yashmal**   يشمل

construct (v, *II*) **yushay-yid**   يشيد

point (v, *IV*) **yusheer**   يشير

become (v, *I*) **yuSbiH**   يصبح

dye (v, *I*) **yaSbigh**   يصبغ

believe (v, *II*) **yuSad-diq**   يصدق

insist (v, *IV doubled*) **yuSirr**   يصر

cry (v, *I*; yell) **yaSrukh**   يصرخ

catch (v, *VIII hollow*; hunt) **yaالسTaad**   يصطاد

fish (v, *VIII hollow*) **yaSTaaD samak**   يصطاد سمك

describe (v, *I assimilated*) **yaSif**   يصف

park (v, *I doubled*; cars, etc.) **yaSuff**   يصف

reach (v, *I assimilated*) **yaSil**   يصل

fix (v, *IV*) **yuSliH**   يصلح

pray (v, *II defective*) **yuSal-lee**   يصلي

design (v, *II*) **yuSam-mim**   يصمم

make; manufacture (v, *I*) **yaSna'**   يصنع

fast (v, *I hollow*) **yaSoom**   يصوم

harass (v, *II*) **yuDaayiq**   يضايق

set (v, *I*; clock, etc.) **yaDbuT**   يضبط

laugh (v, *I*) **yaD-Hak**   يضحك

beat (v, *I*; hit) **yaDrib**   يضرب

put (v, *I assimilated*) **yadaa'**   يضع

join (v, *I doubled;* connect) **yaDumm**	يضم
add (v, *IV hollow*) **yuDeef**	يضيف
cook (v, *I*) **yaTbukh**	يطبخ
deport (v, *I*) **yaTrud**	يطرد
knock (v, *I;* on door, etc.) **yaTruq**	يطرق
feed (v, *IV*) **yuT'im**	يطعم
extinguish (v, *IV*) **yuTfi'**	يطفئ
request (v, *I*) **yaTlub**	يطلب
dial (v, *I*) **yaTlub bit-tilifoon**	يطلب بالتليفون
launch (v, *IV;* new product, etc.) **yuTliq**	يطلق
disinfect (v, *II*) **yuTah-hir**	يطهر
fly (v, *I hollow*) **yaTeer**	يطير
treat (v, *III;* behave towards) **yu'aamil**	يعامل
assist (v, *III*) **yu'aawin**	يعاون
cross (v, *I;* movement) **ya'bur**	يعبر
apologize (v, *VIII*) **ya'tadhir**	يعتذر
count (v, *I doubled;* compute) **ya'idd**	يعد
adjust (v, *II*) **yu'ad-dil**	يعدل
limp (v, *I*) **ya'ruj**	يعرج
show; display; offer (v, *I*) **ya'riD**	يعرض
give (v, *IV defective*) **yu'Tee**	يعطي
know (v, *I*) **ya'lam**	يعلم
teach (v, *II*) **yu'al-lim**	يعلم
return (v, *I hollow*) **ya'ood**	يعود
lend (v, *I hollow*) **yu'eer**	يعير
drown (v, *IV*) **yaghriq**	يغرق

wash (v, I) **yaghsil**	يغسل
cheat (v, I doubled) **yaghishsh**	يغش
cover (v, II) **yughaTTi'**	يغطئ
package (v, II) **yughal-lif**	يغلف
boil (v, I defective; heat) **yaghlee**	يغلي
faint (pass out) **yughma 'alaih**	يغمى عليه
sing (v, II defective) **yughan-nee**	يغني
change (v, II; money, etc.) **yughay-yir**	يغير
fire (v, I; terminate employment) **yafSil**	يفصل
prefer (v, II) **yufaD-Dil**	يفضل
lose (v, I) **yafqid**	يفقد
understand (v, I) **yafham**	يفهم
fight (v, III) **yuqaatil**	يقاتل
accept (v, I) **yaqbal**	يقبل
kill (v, I) **yaqtil**	يقتل
estimate (v, II) **yuqad-dir**	يقدر
read (v, I) **yaqra'**	يقرأ
decide (v, II) **yaqar-rir**	يقرر
divide (v, II) **yuqas-sim**	يقسم
cut (v, I; tear) **yaqTa'**	يقطع
vigilance **yaqDHa**	يقظة
stand (opp. sit); stop (v, I assimilated) **yaqif**	يقف
jump (v, I) **yaqfiz**	يقفز
shut; lock (v, I) **yaqfil**	يقفل
reduce (v, II) **yuqal-lil**	يقلل

fry (v, *I defective*) **yaqlee**	يقلي
say (v, *I hollow*) **yaqool**	يقول
certainty **yaqeen**	يقين
write (v, *I*) **yaktub**	يكتب
repeat (v, *II*) **yukar-rir**	يكرر
hate (v, *I*) **yakrah**	يكره
break (v, *I; smash*) **yaksir**	يكسر
uncover (v, *I*) **yakshif**	يكشف
complement (v, *II; make whole*) **yukam-mil**	يكمل
iron; press (v, *I defective*) **yakwee**	يكوي
wear (v, *I*) **yalbus**	يلبس
heal (v, *VIII; mend*) **yalta'im**	يلتئم
meet (v, *VIII defective*) **yaltaqee**	يلتقي
play (v, *I*) **yal'ab**	يلعب
turn (v, *I doubled; go around*) **yaliff**	يلف
spot (v, *I; see*) **yalmaH**	يلمح
touch (v, *I*) **yalmis**	يلمس
wave (v, *II; with hand*) **yulaw-wiH**	يلوح
compliment (v, *I*) **yamdaH**	يمدح
pass (v, *I doubled; go past*) **yamurr**	يمر
tear (v, *II; shred*) **yumaz-ziq**	يمزق
wipe (v, *I*) **yamsaH**	يمسح
hold; catch (v, *I*) **yamsik**	يمسك
walk (v, *I defective*) **yamshee**	يمشي
fill (v, *I*) **yamla'**	يملأ

have; own (v, I) **yamluk**	يملك
Yemeni **yamaneyy, yamaney-yeen**	يمني
right (opp. left) **yameen**	يمين
call (v, III defective; summon) **yunaadee**	ينادي
sleep (v, I hollow) **yanaam**	ينام
wait (v, VIII) **yantaDHir**	ينتظر
succeed (v, I; opp. fail) **yanjaH**	ينجح
bleed (v, I) **yanzif**	ينزف
slip (v, VII; lose footing) **yanzaliq**	ينزلق
forget (v, I defective) **yansa**	ينسى
join (v, VII doubled; enroll) **yanDamm**	ينضم
look (v, I; see) **yanzhur**	ينظر
organize (v, II) **yunaDH-DHim**	ينظم
refresh (v, IV) **yun'ish**	ينعش
burst (v, VII) **yan-fajir**	ينفجر
save (v, IV; rescue) **yunqidh**	ينقذ
grow (v, I defective) **yanmoo**	ينمو
finish (v, IV defective) **yunhee**	ينهي
intend (v, I defective) **yanwee**	ينوي
land (v, I) **yahbiT**	يهبط
quit (v, I) **yahjur**	يهجر
cross (v, II; interbreed) **yahaj-jin**	يهجن
escape (v, I) **yahrab**	يهرب
mash (v, I) **yahris**	يهرس
Jew(ish) **yahoodeyy, yahood**	يهودي
agree (v, III) **yuwaafiq**	يوافق

deposit (v, *IV*; place securely) **yudi'**	يودع
connect (v, *I*) **yawSil**	يوصل
deliver (v, *II*) **yuwaS-Sil**	يوصل
sign (v, *II*; check, etc.) **yuwaq-qi'**	يوقع
day **yawm, ayaam**	يوم
daily **yawmeyy**	يومي

APPENDIX:

VERB TABLES

INTRODUCTION TO VERBS

Most Arabic verbs have three "root" consonants (non-vowels). There are only two tenses: the *present/future* and the *past.* The person carrying out the action (*I, you, he, she, it,* etc.) is shown by different prefixes and endings around a stem (see table opposite).

Verbs can be one of ten "forms" that are referred to by Latin numerals (e.g. I, II, III, IV, etc.). Form IX has virtually died out in modern Arabic.

There are regular and irregular verbs. Irregular verbs are classified into four main types: *assimilated, hollow, defective* and *doubled.* Verbs are shown in the dictionary under the present tense, third person masculine ("he" form), e.g. **yaktub**. After each verb, you will see a reference, e.g.:

touch (v, *I*) *yalmis*
vanish (v, *VIII defective*) *yakhtafee*

The table(s) on the following pages show how the types of verb are conjugated.

REGULAR VERBS: BASIC FORM I

The vowel before the last root consonant varies in the present tense of regular form I verbs: **yakt<u>u</u>b**, **yaqf<u>i</u>z**. The past is usually vowelled with two "**a**"s between the consonants: **k<u>a</u>t<u>a</u>b**, **q<u>a</u>f<u>a</u>z**.

yaktub *(to write)*	Present/future	Past
ana *(I)*	*a*ktub	katab*t*
	أكتب	كتبت
anta *(you, masc.)*	*ta*ktub	katab*t*
	تكتب	كتبت
anti *(you, fem.)*	*ta*ktub*een*	katab*ti*
	تكتبين	كتبت
huwa *(he)*	*ya*ktub	katab
	يكتب	كتب
hiya *(she)*	*ta*ktub	katab*at*
	تكتب	كتبت
naHnu *(we)*	*na*ktub	katab*na*
	نكتب	كتبنا
antum *(you, pl.)*	*ta*ktub*oon*	katab*tum*
	تكتبون	كتبتم
hum *(they)*	*ya*ktub*oon*	katab*oo*
	يكتبون	كتبوا

REGULAR VERBS: FORMS II–X

The prefixes and endings for forms II–X are the same as form I (see page 189). But the root patterns vary as shown in the table.

	Present/future	*Past*
Form II	**yurat-tib**	**rat-tab**
(to arrange)	يرتّب	رتّب
Form III	**yubaadil**	**baadal**
(to exchange)	يبادل	بادل
Form IV	**yuSliH**	**aSlaH**
(to fix)	يصلح	أصلح
Form V	**yatakal-lam**	**takal-lam**
(to talk/speak	يتكلّم	تكلّم
Form VI	**yatashaajar**	**tashaajar**
(to quarrel)	يتشاجر	تشاجر
Form VII	**yanfajir**	**infajar**
(to burst	ينفجر	انفجر
Form VIII	**yastajim**	**istajam**
(to relax)	يستجم	استجم
Form X	**yastakshif**	**istakshaf**
(to explore)	يستكشف	استكشف

IRREGULAR VERBS: ASSIMILATED

Assimilated verbs are irregular in forms I and VIII. These verbs usually have و (**w**) as their first root consonant. In form I the past tense is regular, but the **w** drops out of the present tense. In form VIII the **w** drops out in both the past and present tenses. Otherwise the endings and prefixes are as regular verbs (see page 189).

	Present/future	Past
Form I	**yaSil**	**waSal**
(to arrive)	يصل	وصل
Form VIII	**yat-taSil**	**it-taSal**
(to contact/call)	يتّصل	اتّصل

IRREGULAR VERBS: HOLLOW

Hollow verbs are so called because the middle root consonant is often replaced by a long or short vowel. There are two main types of hollow verb, those with **oo** in the middle of the present tense, e.g. **yaqool**, and those with a long **ee**, e.g. **yaTeer**. The tables on pages 192–3 show how the two types are conjugated in form I and the table on page 194 covers the other forms.

Hollow verbs: form I (oo)

yaqool *(to say)*	Present/future	Past
ana *(I)*	aqool أقول	qult قلت
anta *(you, masc.)*	taqool تقول	qult قلت
anti *(you, fem.)*	taqooleen تقولين	qulti قلت
huwa *(he)*	yaqool يقول	qaal قال
hiya *(she)*	taqool تقول	qaalat قالت
naHnu *(we)*	naqool نقول	qulna قلبنا
antum *(you, pl.)*	taqooloon تقولون	qultum قلبتم
hum *(they)*	yaqooloon يقولون	qaaloo قالوا

Hollow verbs: form I (ee)

yaTeer (to fly)	Present/future	Past
ana (I)	aTeer أطير	Tirt طرت
anta (you, masc.)	taTeer تطير	Tirt طرت
anti (you, fem.)	taTeereen تطيرين	Tirti طرت
huwa (he)	yaTeer يطير	Taar طار
hiya (she)	taTeer تطير	Taarat طارت
naHnu (we)	naTeer نطير	Tirna طرنا
antum (you, pl.)	taTeeroon تطيرون	Tirtum طرتم
hum (they)	yaTeeroon يطيرون	Taaroo طاروا

Note: There is a third, rarer, group of hollow verbs that have a long **aa** in the middle of the present tense but behave like **yaTeer** in the past tense. The most common of these is the verb **yanaam** (to sleep).

Hollow verbs: forms II–X

Hollow verbs are irregular in forms IV, VII, VIII and X.

	Present/future	*Past*
Form IV	**yureed**	**araad**
(to want)	يريد	أراد
Form VII	**yanhaal**	**inhaal**
(to pour)	ينهال	انهال
Form VIII	**yaHtaaH**	**iHtaaj**
(to need)	يحتاج	احتاج
Form X	**yastareeH**	**istiraaH**
(to rest)	يستريح	استراح

In the past tense, the long **aa** shortens to **a** for **ana** (I), **anta/anti/antum** (you) and **naHnu** (we):

aradt	I wanted
iHtajti	you *(fem.)* needed
istiraHna	we rested

Otherwise the prefixes and endings follow the model in the table on page 189.

IRREGULAR VERBS: DEFECTIVE

Defective verbs end with a vowel in the present tense, either **ee**, **oo**, or **a**. The tables on pages 195–7 show how the three types are conjugated in form I and the table on page 198 covers the other forms.

Defective verbs: form I (ee)

yabkee *(to cry)*	Present/future	Past
ana *(I)*	abkee	bakayt
	أبكي	بكيت
anta *(you, masc.)*	tabkee	bakayt
	تبكي	بكيت
anti *(you, fem.)*	tabkeen	bakayti
	تبكين	بكيت
huwa *(he)*	yabkee	baka
	يبكي	بكى
hiya *(she)*	tabkee	bakat
	تبكي	بكت
naHnu *(we)*	nabkee	bakayna
	نبكي	بكينا
antum *(you, pl.)*	tabkoon	bakaytum
	تبكون	بكيتم
hum *(they)*	yabkoon	bakaw
	يبكون	بكوا

Defective verbs: form I (oo)

yanmoo *(to grow)*	Present/future	Past
ana *(I)*	anmoo	namawt
	أنمو	نموت
anta *(you, masc.)*	tanmoo	namawt
	تنمو	نموت
anti *(you, fem.)*	tanmeen	namawti
	تنمين	نموت
huwa *(he)*	yanmoo	nama
	ينمو	نما
hiya *(she)*	tanmoo	namat
	تنمو	نمت
naHnu *(we)*	nanmoo	namawna
	ننمو	نمونا
antum *(you, pl.)*	tanmoon	namawtum
	تنمون	نموتم
hum *(they)*	yanmoon	namaw
	ينمون	نموا

Defective verbs: form I (a)

yansa *(to forget)*	*Present/future*	*Past*
ana *(I)*	ansa	naseet
	أنسى	نسيت
anta *(you, masc.)*	tansa	naseet
	تنسى	نسيت
anti *(you, fem.)*	tansayna	naseeti
	تنسين	نسيت
huwa *(he)*	yansa	nasiya
	ينسى	نسي
hiya *(she)*	tansa	nasiyat
	تنسى	نسيت
naHnu *(we)*	nansa	naseena
	ننسى	نسينا
antum *(you, pl.)*	tanawn	naseetum
	تنسون	نسيتم
hum *(they)*	yanawn	nasoo
	ينسون	نسوا

Defective verbs: forms II–X

Defective verbs retain their irregularity in all the forms:

	Present/future	Past
Form II *(to pray)*	**yaSal-lee** يصلّي	**Sal-la** صلّى
Form III *(to call/summon)*	**yunaadee** ينادي	**naada** نادى
Form IV *(to finish)*	**yunhee** ينهي	**anha** أنهى
Form V *(to wish)*	**yataman-na** يتمنّى	**taman-na** تمنّى
Form VI *(to meet together*	**yatalaaqa** يتلاقى	**talaaqa** تلاقى
Form VII *(to bend)*	**yanhanee** ينهني	**inhana** انهنى
Form VIII *(to buy)*	**yashtaree** يشتري	**ishtara** اشترى
Form X *(to exclude)*	**yastathnee** يستثني	**istathna** استثنى

All the forms are conjugated like **yabkee** (page 195) except the present tense of forms V and VI which are conjugated like **yansa** (page 197).

IRREGULAR VERBS: DOUBLED

Doubled verbs have the same letter as the second and third root consonant and these usually combine to produce a doubled letter. When an ending is added which begins with a consonant (e.g. **-t** or **-na**), the two root letters separate:

yarudd (to answer)	Present/future	Past
ana *(I)*	arudd أردّ	radadt رددت
anta *(you, masc.)*	tarudd تردّ	radadt رددت
anti *(you, fem.)*	taruddeen تردّين	radadti رددت
huwa *(he)*	yarudd يردّ	rad-da ردّ
hiya *(she)*	tarudd تردّ	rad-dat ردّت
naHnu *(we)*	narudd نردّ	radadna رددنا
antum *(you, pl.)*	taruddoon تردّون	radadtum رددتم
hum *(they)*	yaruddoon يردّون	rad-doo ردّوا

Doubled verbs: forms II–X

The irregular forms of doubled verbs are shown in the table below. The other forms are regular or insignificant. The forms shown below are conjugated like **yarudd** (page 199).

	Present/future	*Past*
Form III *(to oppose)*	**yuDaadd** يضادّ	**Daadd** ضادّ
Form IV *(to like)*	**yuHibb** يحبّ	**aHabb** أحبّ
Form VII *(to enrol)*	**yanDamm** ينضمّ	**inDamm** انضمّ
Form VIII *(to extend)*	**yamtadd** يمتدّ	**imtadd** امتدّ
Form X *(to continue)*	**yastamirr** يستمرّ	**istamarr** استمرّ